INVISIBLE BOUNDARIES:
ADDRESSING SEXUALITIES EQUALITY
IN CHILDREN'S WORLDS

INVISIBLE BOUNDARIES:
ADDRESSING SEXUALITIES EQUALITY
IN CHILDREN'S WORLDS

edited by
Renée DePalma and Elizabeth Atkinson

Trentham Books
Stoke on Trent, UK and Sterling, USA

Trentham Books Limited
Westview House   22883 Quicksilver Drive
734 London Road   Sterling
Oakhill   VA 20166-2012
Stoke on Trent   USA
Staffordshire
England ST4 5NP

First published 2008

British Library Cataloguing-in-Publication Data
A catalogue record for this book is available from the British Library

ISBN: 978 1 85856 430 2

Designed and typeset by Trentham Print Design Ltd, Chester and printed in Great Britain by Cromwell Press Ltd, Trowbridge.

Contents

Acknowledgements

A version of Epstein and Johnson's 'Walking the talk: young people making identities' was given by Debbie Epstein at the 30th Annual Meeting of ANPED in Caxambu, Brasil in October 2007 and will be published in Portuguese as 'Percorrendo a fala: jovens produzindo identidades sexuais' in *Revista Brasileira de Educação.*

The pictures in GLYM ad Frankham's 'A pink rabbit and a blue rabbit: learning about gender (and sex) at primary school' are reproduced with the permission of Change Picture Bank, published by CHANGE, First Floor, 69-85 Old Street, London, EC1V 9HY. http://www.changepeople.co.uk/bank.html.

Aspects of Watkins' 'Heads in the sand, backs against the wall: problems and priorities when tackling homophobia in schools' featured in the 1000 word article 'That thing we *should* talk about' in the Personal, Social, and Health Education magazine *Learning for Life*, September 2006.

A more extended version of DePalma and Atkinson's 'Exploring Gender identity, queering heteronormativity' was published in the *International Journal of Equity and Innovation in Early Childhood*, 5(2) p64-82.

'Using children's literature to challenge homophobia in primary schools' by the *No Outsiders* Project Team appeared in the March 2008 issue of *Books for Keeps: The children's book magazine.*

Whittle, Turner and Al-Alami's 'School: the best days of your life?' was originally published as Chapter 6 in *Engendered Penalties: Transgender and Transsexual People's Experiences of Inequality and Discrimination*, available at www.thee qualitiesreview. org.uk.

Cover art provided by Out for Our Children
The cover art for this book is adapted from a poster entitled *Real Families Rock* produced by the London-based organisation Out for Our Children. They have provided the following brief overview especially for this book:

Who are we?

Out for Our Children is a group of London lesbian parents producing books and resources that reflect our children's lives and family experiences. We think that every child needs love, support and acceptance for who they are and where they come from. Inclusive books and other materials are an essential part of that support.

Our family circumstances and our reasons for having children are as varied as those of any other parents and we are not interested in explaining or justifying to anyone why our families exist. Same-sex parented and LGBT families are a simple fact of life and we are here to stay.

What do we want?

Out for Our Children wants:

- Nurseries, playgroups and schools to welcome our children and celebrate all families

- Children to have a choice of books reflecting real and imaginary lives, including our children's daily realities and aspirations

- A school curriculum which includes us and educates everyone

- Schools and early years settings that work to address and eradicate prejudice and homophobia

What are the issues we face?

The following quotes capture some of our experiences from when our children were very young:

'One of our children had made some little thing at nursery and had written 'for Mummy' on it. And the staff had written below it 'for Mummy and Daddy'! They have sometimes referred to [the partner who less often collects the child] as her nanny.'

'Our son used to go to a parent-run nursery where they knew us really well. But one day they made Diwali cards and they wrote on them 'to Mummy and Daddy'. I was really upset because they knew my child had two mums. I spoke to the staff member and her response was 'Do you want a sticker to cover it over?''

'I remember as a kid having to write 'Mummy and Daddy' [on cards]. I lived in care so I said, 'Why am I doing this? I don't want to do it.' So it's been going on for years.'

'Sometimes when they ask me questions I can tell they've been talking about it for weeks and one of them has been nominated to ask me. Once the question was what does our son call my partner, which I was pleased they asked, but they looked so frightened.'

'Our nursery's policy document used to have lesbian and gay parents mentioned specifically, but the head teacher took it out because he thought we were 'past all that'!'

'I work in primary schools and have found that teachers deal with homophobic language really badly. The response to the use of 'gay' as an insult tends to be either to tell children not to use the word or to tell them that 'gay means happy.' When I've talked about raising it with the children, some teachers have said they're afraid of upsetting religious parents. School staff need training. We ourselves have to practise how to deal with tricky questions in the street, so how are straight teachers supposed to do it? I'd like to see training for teachers involving role play, giving them the opportunity to practice responding to and dealing with the issues.'

What are we doing?
Website: We built a website (www.outforourchildren.co.uk) where parents and educators can find out about the issues, what they can do and how to access resources.

Booklist: We were told that nurseries and primary schools could not find good children's books representing our realities. We looked and we could not find many either! So we decided to hunt across the world and make a booklist. We now have over 50 books on our list from the UK, USA, Spain, Holland and Australia.

Children's Books: We began to write our own children's books, books that we would enjoy reading to our own children. The first two, *Spacegirl pukes* and *If I had A hundred mummies* have been published by Onlywomen Press.

Posters: Our first poster *Real Families Rock*, showing an extended lesbian-parented family, is on display in schools and nurseries across the UK. This is what teachers have said:

- 'Everyone thinks they are great'
- 'They are just perfect'
- 'I think they're fantastic'
- 'What a great poster!'

What will we be doing next?
In Spring 2008 the Equalities and Human Rights Commission awarded us funding (our fifth and largest grant) to employ a worker to develop and extend our work. We will be collaborating with teachers, nursery workers and parents to produce more books and posters and a Teacher's Pack for Foundation Stage education (ages 3-5).

Onwards and upwards ... We are Out for Our Children

Introduction

Renée DePalma and Elizabeth Atkinson

This is a book about making, breaking and contesting boundaries of identity, sexuality and gender. The 'invisible boundaries' we refer to in the title of this book are what separate many children's lived realities from the kinds of adult-constructed realities they might encounter in schools and other adult-run institutions. We focus mainly on schools, perhaps the single most influential institution in children's lives, and the one which has been entrusted with the combined tasks of 'encouraging children to recognise, understand, celebrate and respect similarities and differences between people [and] challenging stereotyping, prejudice and bullying in all its forms ... using materials that show positive images of race, gender, disability and sexual orientation.' (DfES, 2005, p35). In this book we examine some of the obstacles particular to addressing two of these areas of inclusion – gender expression and sexual orientation – and some of the ways in which these obstacles have been challenged.

Sexualities equality concerns the rights of children of lesbian, gay, bisexual and transgender parents, children who may themselves grow up to be LGBT and those who do not conform to gender norms, all of whom frequently experience homophobic bullying. It also concerns heterosexual and gender-traditional children and adults, whose lives are shaped by social norms and constraints, and whose social relations are likely to include encounters with LGBT people. In fact, sexualities equality concerns everyone. Despite its importance in terms of pupil, teacher and community wellbeing, it remains the one area of inclusion still largely unaddressed in schools. We focus on primary schools, families and young children rather than youth or older people because it is in childhood that the foundations for marginalisation are subtly but firmly established. There has been a growing international awareness of the relevance of sexualities equalities to children and the practitioners who work with them. It's been nearly ten years since the US release of Letts and Sears' landmark book *Queering Elementary Education: advancing the dialogue about sexualities and schooling* (1999)[1] and more recently Canadian scholars Isabel Killoran and Karleen Pendleton Jiménez released *Unleashing the Unpopular: talking about sexual orientation and gender diversity in education* (2007). We are pleased to situate this book firmly within this tradition.

Primary schools are not sexually neutral public spaces, although there is a popular tendency to believe that children are asexual beings and that teachers and pupils alike leave their social lives and bodies outside the school gate. Sexual identity is deeply woven into the relationships among pupils and teachers, both in their everyday exchanges and interactions and in the more sinister context of harassment and abuse. Schools are sites of tacit instruction in the possibilities and limitations of gender and sexual identities and within these arenas, heterosexuality and gender conformity are constructed as natural while other sexualities and gendered experiences are silenced. An implicit conceptual link between sexual identity and orientation and sexual activity has led primary teachers to avoid addressing this issue, despite the fact that many children in their care will have some connection to non-heterosexual relationships, and many are likely to identify in later life as lesbian, gay, bisexual or transgender.

'This book arises from a unique series of meetings, also entitled Invisible Boundaries, between researchers, practitioners, interest groups, policy makers and young people who came together between December 2005 and May 2007 to explore children's diverse experiences of lesbian, gay, bisexual and transgender identities in their families, communities, personal lives and schools. Funded by the Economic and Social Research Council (ESRC), these free one-day seminars were held at six universities across England and Wales. Our primary purpose was to bring together researchers, practitioners, interest groups, policy makers and young people to discuss how LGBT issues impact on children and families within and beyond school. The seminars were stimulating and inspiring, and we are indebted to those who presented and those who attended and participated in vital discussions among groups of people who don't always get the chance to talk to each other. The seminar series was designed to enable representatives from various sectors to meet and share ideas about how best to continue to address children's diverse experiences of gender and sexuality in their families, communities, personal lives and schools. The participants whose contributions form the chapters of this book represent a broad cross-section of participants, including parents, researchers, young people, teachers, teacher trainers and activists. Notably, some participants represent two or more of these roles simultaneously.

As convenors of the overall series and coordinators for the University of Sunderland seminar, we would particularly like to recognise the invaluable work of the coordinators at each of the other five participating universities:

> Professor Michael Reiss at the Institute of Education, University of London
>
> Dr. Max Biddulph at the University of Nottingham
>
> Dr. Joanna Frankham at the University of Manchester
>
> Dr. Mark Vicars at the University of Sheffield[2]
>
> Professor Debbie Epstein at the University of Cardiff

In compiling this book, our goals are similar to the original goals of the seminar series:

- to find new ways of conceptualising and overcoming homophobia and transphobia in educational settings

- to share ideas about how to translate policy supporting sexualities equality into the experiences of children and their families

- to include the voices of young LGBT people about their own experiences of childhood

- to provide fresh insights for people working with children in a range of contexts, who may not have had cause to consider the importance and implications of sexualities equality for children's lives

Legislative background to the book

The meetings and discussions which culminated in this book were partially inspired by recent significant UK legislation in relation to sexual identity and social inclusion. Many of our authors, for example, refer to the repeal of Section 28 of the 1988 Local Government Act, which banned 'the promotion of homosexuality as a pretended family relationship.' This legislation, which never actually applied to schools, was finally repealed in 2002 (2000 in Scotland). Nevertheless, Section 28 still casts a lingering shadow of uncertainty about whether it is appropriate or even safe to address sexualities equality in classrooms.

The repeal of Section 28 was followed in 2003 by the Employment Equality (Sexual Orientation) Regulations, which banned discrimination in employment on the grounds of sexual orientation. This has brought many non-heterosexual teachers' long experience of harassment to the public eye. The passing of the Civil Partnership Bill in November 2004 brought about a new era in which the requirement for schools to meet the needs of all their pupils will need to be extended consciously to the needs of pupils from families of from same-sex partnerships. Under the Gender Recognition Act (2004) transgender people can now be legally recognised in their acquired gender, and have a new birth certificate and the right to marry. The Equality Act (2006), which came into force in April 2007, includes a duty to promote gender equality, although it still remains to be seen exactly to what extent this will support protection and inclusion of trans and gender variant people in school settings. At the time of writing (May 2008), the UK House of Commons has voted against a controversial amendment that would require doctors to consider the need for a father when assessing women for fertility treatments. This rejection has been recognised as a significant step for lesbian couples and their children.

In addition, school policy and guidance has begun to demonstrate a commitment to creating genuinely inclusive school environments. Guidance on Sex and Relationships Education includes the recognition of diversity in family relationships (DfEE, 2000). Complementing the publication of *Bullying: Don't Suffer in Silence* (DfES, 2002), the Department or Education and Skills (DfES) later joined forces with the Department of Health (DOH) to demonstrate how addressing homophobia can help schools meet their statutory guidance for student well-being in *Stand Up For Us* (DfES/DOH, 2004). The Government's most recent guidance on embedding anti-homophobic bullying work in schools, *Safe to Learn*, published by the Department for Children, Families and Society (DCSF, 2007) suggests a commitment to preventing rather than simply responding to homophobia in schools. The Behaviour and Attendance and SEAL strands of the Primary National Strategy suggests a proactive approach to curricular inclusion, specifically listing gender and sexual orientation as key areas (DfES, 2005).

Various key educational bodies, including the DfES, The General Council for Teachers in England (GTCE) and Ofsted (the Office for Standards in Education – the official body for inspecting schools in the UK) have expressed a commitment to Stonewall's *Education for All* campaign, a three-year project launched in January 2005 to challenge homophobia in schools. The explicit inclusion of challenges to homophobia in National Anti-Bullying Week (launched in October 2004) and the DfES support for LGBT History Month (launched by Schools OUT in February 2005 and about to celebrate its fifth year) suggest a commitment not just to combating the effects of homophobia but to a proactive policy of inclusion for LGBT people into the curriculum. These government initiatives to foster the inclusion of children and families of diverse sexualities in educational and social contexts will have a serious impact on educational institutions, where homophobia and exclusion persist and in some cases are fuelled by backlash anger, fear and resistance.

Organisation of the book

The book is divided into three sections. Part One, *Policing the boundaries of sex-gender-sexuality in children's worlds*, looks at some of the ways in which invisible boundaries are constructed and maintained for people whose lives do not conform to sex-gender-sexuality norms. Sue Sanders provides a useful starting point by describing some of the ways in which homophobia and transphobia are supported by underlying processes of heteronormativity and sexism in primary schools. She explains how everyday practices, such as the use of the title 'Miss', the appropriation of the term 'gay' (or 'gey') as an insult and the simple assumption that everyone is heterosexual, can contribute to an exclusionary school ethos. Catherine Donovan explores the specific issues faced by children who live in lesbian-headed families and can feel that their own family stories are not included or respected in school spaces. She challenges primary schools to provide a positive environment in which a diversity of family stories is understood as ordinary. Whittle, Turner and Al-Alami share some results from a major research project on transgender and transsexual people's experiences of inequality and discrimination in the UK. Respondents recalled that in addition to intense experiences of bullying and harassment, gendered school practices such as uniforms and sport contributed to their sense of alienation. Debbie Epstein and Richard Johnson examine how socially and institutionally-defined power relations can contribute to the development of pathologised identities in terms of sexuality and gender.

In Part Two, *Memories of transgressive childhoods*, we first hear from a group of young people about the effects of withholding knowledge from children about same-sex attraction. Together with Jo Frankham, young people from Gay and Lesbian Youth Manchester help us to understand how their early experiences with implicit gender and behaviour norms constructed their own childhoods as transgressive. Claire Jenkins evokes images of her childhood as an institutionally-determined boy and reflects on her path from the official birth registration as 'boy' to legal and social renegotiation of her sexual identity as an adult woman. Mark Vicars tells the story of John, whose early attempts to understand and express his emerging sexuality were unsupported by the schools he attended. Through the eyes of John's parents we see how John became increasingly alienated from the school communities, who tended to see him as the source of the problem.

We turn to action and possibilities for critical, informed school practice in Part Three, *Schools as sites for contesting boundaries*. Kate Hinton shows us how family and school staff worked to provide a supportive environment for J, a gender variant child, in both primary and secondary settings. This story does not pretend that everyone was sure of themselves all the time, but it does show how open minds and the willingness to work together can make a significant difference. Jay Stewart (the only contributing author who was not part of the original seminar series) provides a commentary on J's story. His insights place the story in the broader context of trans and gender variant experiences and ways in which these identities might be might be better supported by schools and other institutions.

Mara Sapon-Shevin takes a wider look at inclusion as an aspect of school culture relevant to all pupils. This chapter provides specific examples of how songs, books and role play activities can help foster socially just classroom communities. Also concentrating on classroom practice, David Watkins draws upon examples from his own experience as a teacher of children with learning difficulties. He discusses ways in which school staff can be supported in incorporating discussions about homosexuality into their curriculum. Renée DePalma and Elizabeth Atkinson (the editors of this book) demonstrate how sexual identity, gender performance and sexuality tend to become entangled in primary school contexts, despite the fact that they are actually very different aspects of human experience. Drawing upon their research at the primary level, they argue that an understanding based on raising questions and troubling normative categories can help us to understand and challenge heteronormative processes in schools. Finally, the *No Outsiders* Project Team (of which DePalma and Atkinson are members) provides an overview of ways in which primary teachers in the project have used a range of books to create opportunities for sexuality and gender-based inclusion in primary schools throughout England, as part of their exploration of strategies to address sexualities equality in their own schools and classrooms.

With the publication of this collected volume, we hope to share what we know and have learned with anyone living or working with children: parents, teachers, community workers, voluntary workers, and all those brought under the broad scope of children's services across the UK and equivalent services elsewhere. We aim to bring together the voices of people who realise the urgency of addressing issues of sexualities and gender equality at the earliest possible point in young children's lives. In a world where, in the words of the UK government, *Every Child Matters* (DfES, 2004), it is crucial that we recognise that there are no exceptions.

References
Department for Children, Schools and Families (2007) *Safe to Learn: Embedding anti-bullying work in schools.* London: DCSF

Department for Education and Employment (2000) *Sex and Relationship Guidance*. London: Department for Education and Employment

Department for Education and Skills (2002) *Bullying: Don't Suffer in Silence*. London: DfEE

Department for Education and Skills (2004) *Every Child Matters: Next Steps*. London: DfES

Department for Education and Skills (2005) *Social and emotional aspects of learning: Primary National Strategy*. London: DfES

Department of Education and Skills and Department of Health (2004) *Stand up for Us: Challenging Homophobia in Schools*. London: DfES and Department of Health

Killoran, I and Jiménez, K (eds). (2007) *Unleashing the Unpopular: talking about sexual orientation and gender diversity in education*. Olney, MD: Association for Childhood Education International

Letts, W and Sears, J (eds) (1999) *Queering elementary education: advancing the dialogue about sexualities and schooling*. Lanham, MD: Rowman and Littlefield

Notes

1 One of our chapter authors, Mara Sapon-Shevin, was a contributor to this edited volume.

2 Mark has since taken a Senior Lecturer post at the University of Victoria, Melbourne, Australia.

PART ONE:
Policing the boundaries of sex-gender-sexuality in children's worlds

1

Tackling homophobia, creating safer spaces

Sue Sanders

Sanders is co-Chair of Schools OUT, which campaigns, educates, and lobbys for equality in education for lesbian, gay, bisexual and trans people. Based on the premise that equality requires a change of culture in society and, more particularly, the culture of our schools and colleges, Schools OUT seeks to address issues of equality through both the legislative/regulative and cultural routes, as they mutually reinforce each other. Here Sanders provides an overview of the ways in which hetero-sexism, homophobia, sexism and transphobia operate together in schools, describes ways in which legislation supports addressing these problems, and outlines some of the resources and support available for teachers who want to make a difference. This chapter provides an over-view of the ways in which the boundaries of sex-gender-sexuality are policed within and beyond schools. The other chapters in Parts One and Two focus more specifically on how these processes operate, while Part Three takes up more specifically some of Sanders' suggestions for action. In his chapter, David Watkins describes some of the ways he, as a teacher, has put some of these suggestions into practice.

Lesbians, gay men, bisexual and trans people are Black, White, dual-heritage, daughters, sons, aunts, mothers, sisters, brothers, fathers, uncles, nephews, nieces, friends, colleagues, workers, non-waged, students, teachers, customers, non-disabled, Jewish, Hindu, Sikh, Muslim, Christian, of all religions and none, old and young, women and men, live in both rural and urban areas and represent every political perspective.

This is probably the most important thing I say when I go into schools. I do a lot of training in schools and I refuse to work with young people until I've worked with the staff. My experience is that if you work with young people in schools before you've prepared the staff you're actually making more problems than you're solving. We need to give our teachers the confidence and competence to deal with this work.

So this statement is the one which begins to get people thinking. When I say to staff, 'Tell me about the lesbian, gay, bisexual and transgender people you know', they're always White and they're always male. There might be the odd lesbian, and certainly not transgender. When I come out as a lesbian to young people in the classroom and I give them the evaluation sheets I say, 'Is there anything in the session that surprised you?' I consistently get, 'That that old woman was a dyke'. Apparently you can't be old and a lesbian, either. Very often when I go to LGBT conferences there is a paucity of Black and Asian people as speakers and our Schools OUT committee was entirely White till 2008. It's something that we worked very hard to change.

My passion is to enable people to recognise that homophobia sits on heterosexism, which is a set of assumptions and practices that promotes heterosexual relationships as the only 'natural' and valid form of sexual orientation. Heterosexism recognises and rewards those who are heterosexual and ignores and penalises those who are not. It's extraordinary to go into places like the Crime Prosecution Service and find police officers who know what heterosexism means. It's amazing! That's not always true of teachers, because teachers are not getting the same sort of level of training as police officers around diversity and power relationships. This is kind of weird, but we do have to thank Doreen Lawrence[1] for an enormous amount of this. The landscape changed profoundly after the Stephen Lawrence Inquiry, profoundly. The criminal justice system really grabbed the Inquiry team and began thinking through, 'Well, hang on, there's such a thing as institutional discrimination and oppression.' So, ironically, when I'm working in the criminal justice system, I get lots of nods, but often when I'm working in the education system it comes as a bit of a shock. But our schools are profoundly institutionally heterosexist. All our schools assume everyone's heterosexual unless you put up your hand and wave.

I was at Oxford University recently for a big national Student Pride event. And there were probably about 200 to 250 students there and I said, 'OK, put your hands up those of you who had out and proud members of staff in your school.' Four hands went up. Now, that is an indictment of our system. It's an indictment of the fact that the DfES (Department for Education and Skills, replaced in 2007 by Department for Children, Schools and Families – DCSF) is not in any way, shape or form sending messages to LGBT staff that they welcome them and celebrate them and recognise what an enormous amount of work they're doing. Ironically, the police do. If anybody had told me 20 years ago that I'd be singing the praises of the police, I'd have had conniptions.

They've just done a mini-report coming from the Stephen Lawrence Inquiry. And what they've discovered from looking up and down the country is that racism has dropped considerably within the force, but they're now spotting sexism and heterosexism, which is terribly exciting. They're actually recognising it and saying, 'Yes, there's lots more work to do'. But the police actually do have lesbian, gay, bisexual and transgender liaison officers, and they actually have advisory groups. I'm a member of one with the Metropolitan police, where a whole lot of lesbian, gay, bisexual and transgender people yell at them and tell them what to do, and sometimes they do it, whereas in education, we haven't started that process at all yet. And I have been talking to the DfES and told them, 'Go and talk to the police. Go and learn from them.' It seems to me that it's really crucial to get people to understand just how heterosexist our schools are.

One of the tools of heterosexism is what I get called as soon as I move into a school – 'Hello, Miss!' I get so angry. Isn't it interesting that unmarried women are called 'Miss'? We've missed something. And I constantly say, 'I have missed nothing. Don't you call me 'Miss!' Isn't it interesting, how our language does that? That's heterosexism, every day on the minute, on every person's lips all the time. There are some schools where teachers call each other 'Miss', which I find even more offensive. I will be called 'politically correct' for this but as far as I'm concerned 'PC' also stands for 'professional competence' and I'm very proud to be both politically correct and professionally competent.

Schools haven't really decided what homophobia is, so they might be trying to deal with something (maybe) without having quite decided what it is. The Metropolitan Police definition of a homophobic incident is a real gift:

- Any incident which is perceived to be homophobic by the victim or another person

- that is directed to impact upon those known or perceived to be lesbian, gay, bisexual or trans people

Basically what it says is, 'It is if anyone says it is'. And we treat it as such. Now if we could get our schools to take that on board as a definition I think we would be moving a long way. It's adapted from a definition of racism, but the second paragraph is absolutely crucial, because we all know that you don't have to be LGBT to be homophobically bullied. I'm getting a lot of calls from lesbian mums whose children are going through hell, and the school is blaming the mums.

Here is what's happening to our young people in schools. This is what they're facing:

- Sixty-five percent of lesbian and gay pupils have experienced homophobic bullying

- Of those, 92 percent (143,000) have experienced verbal homo-phobic bullying, 41 percent (64,000) physical bullying and 17 percent (26,000) death threats

- 97 percent of gay pupils hear derogatory phrases such as 'dyke', 'queer' and 'rug-muncher' used in school

- Half of teachers fail to respond to homophobic language when they hear it

- Thirty percent of lesbian and gay pupils say that adults – teachers or support staff – are responsible for homophobic incidents in their school

- Less than a quarter of schools have told pupils that homo-phobic bullying is wrong (Hunt and Jensen, 2007)

What we need to be thinking about is not just tackling homophobia. This is what's happening to our LGBT students, or students who are assumed to be LGBT. But it is indicative of the power relationship young people have with each other, and the bullying culture that exists in our schools. And I am passionate about the fact that although I'm trying to eradicate homophobia, what I am actually saying is: we have to eradicate that whole process and that whole culture which gives credence to somebody treating somebody else badly because of who they are. Full stop.

So while we have to highlight homophobia, because it's something that people consistently forget, we cannot tackle homophobia on its own. We have to be dealing with racism, sexism, heterosexism, size-ism, you know, whatever it is that kids have a go at each other on. That's the thing we actually have to look at. What is in our culture which is constantly enabling and often condoning people treating each other badly?

What are the costs of homophobia?

- ■ Alcohol and drug misuse – blocking out the pain

- ■ Truancy as students seek to escape from the persecution

- ■ Giving up on academic achievement as students find they are unable to work effectively in their environment

- ■ Suffering from emotional, mental and/or physical health conditions, such as eating disorders, as a result of the anxiety and eroded self esteem

- ■ Promiscuous sexual practices leading to early pregnancies due to confusion and internalised homophobia

Now I could have described these things as 'behaviours of LGBT people', but I deliberately called it 'The costs of homophobia' because I am sick to death of careless language such as, 'Oh, that Black boy who was standing at the bus stop was murdered because he was Black.' No he wasn't. He was murdered because of racism. Everything I listed are coping strategies of people who are bullied. It is not because they're lesbian and gay, not because they're girls, not because they're Asian, not because they're fat or because they wear glasses, but because of the bullying behaviour. That's what we need to tackle.

The costs of homophobia are very high, and because governments haven't been thinking about the issue, they keep going up. So what's extraordinary is that there have been huge amounts of government money spent on tackling alcohol and drug misuse. Have they looked at homophobia? No. Millions of pounds were spent a couple of years ago on truancy, but did they ever look at homophobia? No. In the whole area of emotional and physical health conditions, eating disorders and all the rest of it, did they ever look at homophobia? It's pretty obvious.

We have research now which makes it clear that young lesbian and gay teenagers get involved in either having babies or causing babies. What's going on? They're trying to fit in, trying to say, 'I'm not gay', either to themselves or to other people. At the party, you're drunk and everybody else is pairing off. You're even less likely to have prepared your contraception than everybody else, and suddenly you're pressurised into something. We have a very high proportion of pregnancies involving lesbian and gay teens. But is homophobia taken into account around dealing with unwanted pregnancy? Never been thought of in this country – outrageous!

Take the issue of homelessness. A high proportion of our young people get thrown out of homes. Do we deal with that? Why aren't we picking these young people up? If we do pick them up we send them straight back to the place they've run away from. Is that helpful?

Obviously the issues around young LGBT children are problematic: Where are the services for them? Where are we talking about them? Where are the words mentioned? But if you are Black and LGBT, if you're Asian and LGBT, if you're disabled, your chances of experiencing homophobic violence are even greater. If you have a mobility problem, for example, you are dependent upon somebody else to get you to that one LGBT youth club. Think of all the commercial LGBT clubs there are in London. Two of them are fully accessible. That's such an indictment of our community. Why aren't we thinking about this issue? When we were preparing the events for LGBT History Month we eventually had to pay someone to work virtually full-time to go to everybody who was setting up events and make them fill in the disability access forms. Sure they're complicated – of course they are. We've got to think through how we make venues accessible to everybody. But it's a big issue. If we're serious about inclusion, if we're screaming about, 'What about us?' then we've also got to start thinking, 'Well, what about all of us?' We need to think about whether we are being inclusive within our own community. When we design services for LGBT people, are we thinking across the whole spectrum of LGBT youth, or are we only thinking about predominantly White people, and possibly predominantly White boys?

Hazel Wallace (2005) did research in 2004 and compared some of her findings with Loraine Trenchard and Hugh Warren's (1984) ground-breaking work. Wallace found that more young people are being rejected by family members on disclosure of sexual orientation but fewer are being thrown out of home. Those who remain at home can face violence from family members. Over half the respondents who reported experiencing violence from family members due to their sexual orientation still lived at home and two thirds had been bullied at school.

Now the word we hear everywhere is 'gay' which apparently, according to an article in the *Times Educational Supplement* (Lowrison, 2006) is spelled 'g-e-y' and has nothing to do with homophobia. That's something I consistently find when I go around schools and I work with teachers and with young people: they will all sit there and tell me, 'Oh, no, we're not having a go, no, no, we're not being homophobic, it's just a word, isn't it?' I say, 'OK, well, actually you're celebrating me, aren't you? And if you change the word from 'gay' to 'Jew', 'spaz' or 'Black' would you be comfortable with that?' Little bells begin to go. A few flickers of eyelids as they begin to think, 'Oh, maybe not.' So it seems to me it's something that we really rigorously have to challenge. Maybe as the *Times Educational Supplement* would see it, I've just got the spelling wrong.

How are we equipping our teachers to deal with this? I had one teacher come up to me, very proud and very excited, and say, 'Oh, I've solved the problem, Sue, none of that happens now. We don't let the word 'gay' be mentioned at all in the classroom.' I kind of feel, well, at least they're trying, but they haven't thought it through. Where's the training? Where's the support for them to actually think about what young LGBT people want? For a start:

- to be provided with a safe and supportive environment free from discrimination and prejudice

- to be able to come in confidence to teachers who will understand that coming out is both important and positive

- to be supported if they choose to come out

- for teachers to actively challenge homophobia and transphobia wherever it occurs

- for LGBT and other young people to see positive images and hear positive messages about lesbian, gay, bisexual and transgender people

One of the really interesting things is getting people to think about how they will deal with young people coming out to them. I do a bit of role play to get people to think about it because I don't want the classic: 'oh, I don't know very much about that, but I know a counsellor who does'. This immediately medicalises matters. Some disabled people are challenging our thinking about oppression and the way it works. There's the medical model, where I go to a doctor, who tries to cure me and sort me out and find ways of looking after me. Then there's the social model, which looks at the barriers that make it impossible for me to access the world as a disabled person. As a diversity trainer, I'm working on getting people to think about the social model. My perception is that when people talk about LGBT they are definitely using the medical model. And it wasn't until about 1990, as a consequence of how the United Nations and World Health Organisation sorted themselves out, that I ceased having a medical disease. That was only 16 years ago.

We have a long history of being illegal, and men have had it even worse. It wasn't until 2001 that we were granted equal age of consent. Section 28 has only just been scrapped. So we have this whole bulk of stuff that's been telling us and the world that LGBT people are, well, to coin a phrase, queer. Diseased, criminals, different, pederasts; we do nasty things to ourselves and to other people. There are lots of stereotypes out there that are really unpleasant. Black people are frequently treated as Other; women, well, where do I start? All these groups have been treated as if they are the problem and it is they who have to adapt to society. The social model is saying what we need to do is to look at the barriers which dis-enable people to be effective and to be able to utilise the whole of society. I'm trying to get people to recognise that the issue is dealing with homophobia and heterosexism, not problematising LGBT people or Black people or disabled people or women or older or younger people. It's turning it round and saying, 'What are we doing that dis-enables people to be functioning effectively?'

This year the Teacher Support Network did an online piece of research which discovered that 60 percent of teachers were being homophobically or transphobically bullied. The biggest perpetrators were pupils, followed by colleagues, managers and pupils' parents. Only a quarter of schools had a code of conduct on homophobic, biphobic and transphobic behaviour but in 65 percent of cases, the policy was not properly enforced. We have yet to hear what the DfES are going to do about that.

We have legislation now which helps us. According to the Skills and Learning Act (2000) and Sex and Relationship Guidance (2000), teachers need to:

■ challenge the stigmatisation of lesbian and gay families in lessons about families, marriage and stable relationships

■ give positive information on lesbians, gays and bisexuals to enable pupils to challenge derogatory stereotypes and prejudice

■ include lesbian, gay and bisexuality in lessons on sex education

■ challenge all forms of homophobic bullying

Ofsted (the Office for Standards in Education, Children's Services and Skills, which inspects and regulates UK schools) now includes addressing homophobic bullying in the inspection of schools. Now these documents have been around for six years, but not many people seem to be familiar with them. They just haven't been communicated effectively.

Wednesday May 17 was International Day Against Homophobia. Fifty countries around the world celebrated, challenged, and looked at the whole issue of tackling homophobia. We're very lucky. We can sit in a university and talk about homophobia. There are certain countries where you can still be shot because you're lesbian or gay. We need to acknowledge that. We also need to do something about the appalling situation of gay and lesbian asylum seekers coming over to this country and getting no support.

Until recently, most LGBT people preferred to avoid attention. Many still do. Even today, the penalties for those who refuse to conceal themselves, or fail to do so, can be severe. They can range from ostracism and victimisation to assault and even murder. LGBT History Month, which was initiated by Schools OUT in February 2005 and will take place every February, seeks to rectify this situation. This is an opportunity for all of us to learn more about the histories of lesbian, gay, bisexual and transgender people. LGBT History Month is about identity. It's about us as people. Discrimination in schools isn't just about being nasty to us. It is ignoring us and making us invisible in schools. By changing the curriculum of our schools we can make schools safe and comfortable places for all who use them, and provide an appropriate education for all our students.

To find out more about Schools OUT, visit our website at http://www.schools-out.org.uk/

More information about LGBT History month is available at www.lgbthistorymonth.org.uk

Note

1 Doreen Lawrence is the mother of Stephen Lawrence, the victim of a brutal racially motivated murder in south east London. The Stephen Lawrence Inquiry subsequently defined institutional racism as 'the collective failure of an organisation to provide an appropriate and professional service to people because of their colour, culture or ethnic origin' (Macpherson, 1999).

References

Department for Education and Employment (2000) *Sex and Relationship Guidance.* London: DfEE

Hunt, R and Jensen, J (2007) *The School Report: the experiences of young gay people in Britain's schools.* London: Stonewall http://www.stonewall.org.uk/education_ for_all/research/1790.asp (July 2007)

Lowrison, D (2006) You talking to me? *Times Educational Supplement,* 12 May. http://www.tes.co.uk/search/story/?story_id=2234062 (January 2008)

Macpherson, W *et al* (1999) *The Stephen Lawrence Inquiry.* London: The Stationary Office

Trenchard, L and Warren, H (1984) *Something To Tell You.* London: London Gay Teenage Group

Wallace, H (2005) *Time to Think* http://calm-seas.co.uk/timetothink/ (January 2008)

2

Feeling at home: children of lesbian-headed families telling their family stories in primary school settings

Catherine Donovan

This chapter explores research about primary-aged children living in lesbian-headed families to discuss factors influencing the extent to which children are able to tell their family stories openly in primary schools. Together with Whittle, Turner and Al-Alami's perspective of the experiences of children with trans parents, the chapters illustrate the important role for primary schools in providing a positive space in which children can talk about their families. However, in deciding how to translate this responsibility into reality, schools should acknowledge the different ways children deal with telling their family story and what influences them: for example, how their lesbian-headed family has been formed; how parents prepare their children to cope with potentially hostile and always curious others. Donovan provides a preliminary agenda for change for primary schools to provide a positive environment in which a diversity of family stories is understood as ordinary, an agenda which is taken up by the *No Outsiders* project team in their chapter about children's literature.

Introduction

For lesbian, gay, bisexual and queer (LGBQ) people in the UK, the new millennium has seen the legal and social landscape transformed in favour of their status as citizens and as parents creating families. The Adoption and Fostering Act (2002) and The Civil Partnership Act (2004) are just two examples of the ways in which people in same-sex relation-ships wanting or having children have been provided with the same rights and responsibilities as those enjoyed by heterosexual couples in marriage. Yet there is evidence that the social status of people in same-sex relationships or LGBQ-headed families has not yet caught up with existing legal equalities. A key area where this is the case is in our schools, and this has serious implications for children growing up in such families. This chapter explores the ways in which primary-aged children in these families are supported by their primary schools to tell their family story – or not. Although there is some relevance for other families this chapter concentrates on experiences of lesbian-headed families.

The chapter is divided into three sections. The first provides a brief his-tory of the emergence of lesbian headed families in the UK and some of the key differences between families that can affect the kinds of family stories children might tell in primary school settings. In the second sec-tion there is an outline of the research that has been done on lesbian-headed families, and discussion of some relevant key findings. Finally, some conclusions are drawn about how the families and primary schools can facilitate children feeling that their family stories can be told and respected in the school setting.

The context

Looking back over the last thirty years one can see a seismic shift in the possibilities for living openly as a lesbian in the UK. The repeal of Section 28 across the UK and the proactive government support for anti-homophobic bullying campaigns[1] suggests that inequalities based on sexuality are beginning to be addressed in schools. The clearest statement of this is found in the Department for Education and Em-ployment's *Sex and Relationship Guidance* (2000) (hereafter the HFeS Guidance) albeit in a somewhat contradictory way. The introduction to the HFeS Guidance states, with no little pride, that the document is the first national framework for the development of work in sex and relationship education. It is quickly established that this framework is both grounded on, and aims to promote (heterosexual) marriage but the document acknowledges that other kinds of relationships exist which must also be respected and protected from stigmatisation:

> As part of sex and relationship education, pupils should be taught about the nature and importance of marriage for family life and bringing up children. But the Government recognises ... that there are strong and mutually supportive relationships outside marriage. Therefore pupils should learn the significance of marriage *and stable relationships* as key building blocks of community and society. Care needs to be taken to ensure that there is no stigmatisation of children based on their home circumstances. (HFeS Guidance, 2000, p4, *my emphasis*)

Whilst the document can be understood as an attempt to acknowledge and promote tolerance of family diversity, it is clear that heterosexual marriage is to be promoted at the top of a hierarchy of relationships. Nevertheless, the HFeS Guidance clearly provides a lead for schools to ensure that all the families from which their children come be acknowledged and shown respect. For the children from lesbian-headed families, this document provides the opportunity for their experiences of school, both before and after they tell their family story, to be positive and inclusive. The HFeS Guidance is therefore important as it requires schools to develop policies of inclusiveness about the different kinds of families of their children.

Along with these social, legal and cultural shifts, a shift has occurred in the ways in which LGBQ people present themselves. From the 1950s to the 1980s the focus of much literature and activism from LGBQ people was focused on their rights as individuals to exist, come out and live as LGBQ. From the 1980s onwards we have seen these stories widening out from the individual to the couple and the family. Concerns are no longer limited to individual identity but embrace relationships. In the biggest study of the intimate and family lives of LGBQ people in the UK to date, Weeks *et al* (2001) talked about the ways in which families of choice are being constructed that include some but not necessarily all of their families of origin, friends and ex-lovers, their children and their partners, and that these families of choice engage in many of the practices of heterosexual nuclear families but with less sense of duty and greater sense of negotiated responsibility (Finch and Mason, 1993).

Many of the respondents in this study had children. Weeks *et al* (2001) identified three key ways in which children and parenting were talked about. In stories of impossibilities, gay men in particular talk about living at a time and in a place where children and homosexuality are incompatible. Sometimes gay men and lesbians marry in order to have the children they desire but most tell stories of forgoing their desire for children so they can live as non-heterosexual people. In stories of opportunities, lesbians particularly speak about having children in heterosexual relationships and then coming out and feeling that it was possible to continue parenting as an out lesbian. In stories of choice, lesbians mainly, but gay men too, talk about the ways they feel they can be open in their sexuality and opt into parenthood through using donor or self-insemination, adoption or fostering, surrogacy and so on. These stories can be understood to represent particular times in our recent history but they should also be understood as existing simultaneously depending on where people live and what resources they can tap for living as openly LGBQ people.

The stories about parenting describe non-heterosexual parents and children whose different family experiences shape the ways in which their family stories can be told. For example, Weeks *et al* (2001) suggested that children who have previously lived in a heterosexual-headed family may experience their current lesbian-headed family in terms of loss: loss of their previous family home and relationships and loss of their father as a live-in parent. Research indicates that children from divorced families living with a lesbian mother (with or without a female partner) are more likely to continue a regular relationship with their father than those coming from divorced families with a heterosexual mother (Golombok, Spencer and Rutter, 1983). However, the existence of a father and his family present particular kinds of issues that can affect the ways in which the lesbian-headed family and the mother's partner are perceived both within and beyond the family and will therefore influence the family story children feel they can tell.

For children growing up with lesbian parents (who live singly or in couples) who have planned their family there is no sense of loss of a previous family or living situation but there will be a growing sense of difference from other families, particularly in relation to questions of who and where their father is and how the non-biological parent is explained. In addition, LGBQ families who have used a known donor to conceive may have an involved father or fathers and their family networks will also be accommodated within the children's family story. So it is of some importance that lesbian-headed families are understood to be characterised by difference rather than homogeneity.

The existing research

Most of the research on non-heterosexual headed families focuses on lesbian-headed families and compares (usually) the psychological outcomes for children from these families with those from heterosexual families (see Tasker, 2005 for an overview). What this research shows is that children's well being and adaptation depends not on the sexuality of their parents but on the quality of the familial relationships (eg Patterson, 2006); and familial relationships are positively associated with the parents' openness with the children about their sexuality, especially if this is done before adolescence and with the involvement of their partners (eg Oswald, 2002).

The other type of research conducted with lesbian-headed families has been more sociological and anthropological, exploring how they understand and make sense of their own family, parenting and kin relationships. In common with most other research in the field, these studies are small-scale, involving respondents who are mainly White and well resourced financially, materially and educationally. Consequently, Gabb (2004) urges caution that we do not assume that these families represent all families headed by non-heterosexuals.

However, some of the qualitative work done with lesbian-headed families does provide starting points for discussion about how primary schools might provide an environment in which the children of LGBQ-headed families could feel positive about telling their family story. As well as recognising the diversity of experience in lesbian-headed families it is also important to recognise that the children of these families will have various ways of presenting themselves and their families in school and to school friends and that these approaches will change over time and even vary between siblings.

The work of Weeks *et al* (2001) suggests that parents are aware that their children inhabit spheres of living that are separate from that of the family: the school, the playground, spaces and times with their friends. And these spheres are recognised as being places in which children take the lead in how they talk about and present their family story. This is particularly important for children who originated within heterosexual relationships and for whom relationships with biological fathers and female co-parents may not be straightforward. Here, for example is Jane explaining an incident at a primary school concerning her daughter:

> [My 7-year old daughter has told] most of her close friends ... about me and Margaret [Jane's partner], you know, it's not been a problem. But there was a little lass in the line as we took them to school one morning – that she's had a few arguments with in the past and [she] can be quite lippy – and this little lass said, 'who's that then?' So she said, 'that's my mummy, my mummy'. And she said 'No, that person with your mummy?' And she said, 'Oh, she's ... she's a friend of mine, a friend of mum's'. And it's like, you know we chatted about it afterwards. She said 'Mum was that all right?' and I said, 'well it's fine, you know, we're quite happy to be whatever you explain us to be. Because you know your friends a lot better than we do. So you say what's comfortable and we'll go along with that.' (Weeks *et al*, 2001, p175-176)

The issue here was not 'who is your father?' but 'who is this other person who brings you to school?' Tasker and Golombok found that children of the lesbian mothers in their study were more positive about their families when they felt a sense of control over who knew about their mothers being lesbian (in Oswald, 2002). There is also evidence that co-parents will refrain from involving themselves with schools if the children have any anxiety about being exposed as coming from a lesbian-headed family (*ibid*). This is more often the case with children who originate in heterosexual relationships (Lindsay *et al*, 2006).

Lesbian parents often allow their children the freedom to take their time and find friends they can trust to tell, and prepare their children by rehearsing with them what kinds of stories they can tell and reassuring them that they, the children, can control who, when and what they tell (Gartrell *et al*, 1996; 2005; Lindsay *et al*, 2006). Donovan and Wilson (2008) found evidence of parents striving to provide their children with strategies and/or skills for negotiating school life. Sue and Kay illustrate this:

> **Sue:** We say you've got two Mummies which is interesting because David calls Kay Mummy and calls me Sue. Yvonne calls me Mummy but she calls Kay 'Katy' ... when we go to school, because David started at school this year ... they always refer to whichever one of us is picking him up as 'your Mummy's here.' So he's kind of got used to the fact that, with outside people...

Kay: You know [he has said] 'they called Sue Mummy today' and I said, 'well you know, she isn't your Mummy, I'm your Mummy but she's like a Mummy isn't she? And if you want to say she's your Mummy that's fine. If you want to say 'she's not my Mummy, she's Suzy' then say that but you must say what you want to say, it's entirely your story.' (*ibid*, p23-24)

This excerpt reflects the skills parents try to impart to their children: that they don't have to talk to people about these things – they are private and not necessarily other people's business; that they should not tell lies about their family; that they can take the lead in how and to whom they want to tell their family story.

Similarly, Janet explains how she and her partner Lianne responded when their 7-year old son got himself into a 'pickle' after he let his friends think that a family friend was his father, 'What we have said to Geoff is that it was completely up to him, as long as he didn't lie and get into difficulties, who he told and we would never tell anybody, we would always take the lead from him.'

Janet and Lianne talk about preparing their children with possible ways of avoiding questions about their family when they feel uncomfortable about answering, or 'how to be evasive without being noticeable and how to change the subject if you are not wanting to get into [it]'. Since these strategies can result in the denial of a loved other parent, we can also see that schools can help, not necessarily by getting involved with the individual children – who may not want to be singled out for special treatment or be mortified by teachers knowing their business – but by creating an environment in which the diversity of family life is part of the way they approach their curriculum.

At the same time, most lesbian parents are concerned that their children feel positive about their family and believe it is the adults' responsibility to nurture a sense of pride in it. Children of women who have opted into parenthood as out lesbians are often told stories about how much their parents wanted children and sought out known donors, clinics or adoption agencies to help them have the children they so wanted. For those who have come out since having children in heterosexual relationships it is important that they are honest with their children about the nature of their lesbian relationship and the role of the mother's lesbian partner in the family. Jane explains here how she felt she had to be honest with her children so that they would feel positive about the family relationships they have since Jane split up with their father:

> The other day she came home [from school] and she said '[my friend] says mummies aren't supposed to have girlfriends'. I said 'Ah, did he?' [laughs] thinking 'oh shit here we go'. And she said 'yeah, but I said 'well it doesn't matter does it, if you love someone, whether it's a girl or a boy as long as you love each other' ... and he said 'oh I suppose you're right.' ... I couldn't not be out to them I don't think. I think they need to feel that I think it's fine and I'm not ashamed – to be able to deal with the shit that they inevitably will get. And certainly they feel very confident in us as a relationship and so they do feel, you know if somebody does say something that they'd say 'oh that's just rubbish. It's not like that actually.'

Lesbian parents are sensitive to the potential for their children to experience homophobia at primary school and take steps to prevent this in their choice of school, trying to select multicultural and diverse schools and contacting the school administration early in their children's school career (Lindsay *et al*, 2006). A recent study in Australia of the experiences of lesbian mothers and their children in primary and secondary schools found that the children's experiences at primary school were more positive than at secondary school and confirmed that the children who had more positive experiences at school had parents who had been out with the school from the start (Lindsay *et al*, 2006). Children's strategies for telling their family stories (or coming out as it is put in this study) were heavily influenced by their parents' strategies, teachers' responses, peer responses and age (*ibid*). However, the strategies of children were not static and were contingent on their most recent experiences. 'Homophobia created wariness and positive responses created openness ... children in particular displayed a watchful approach that allowed change and adaptability' (Lindsay *et al*, 2006, p1074).

Children make their decisions according to whether they feel they can trust their peers and whether telling the truth will create negative consequences for them. One 10-year old interviewed for the Families of Choice project explains how and why she makes the decisions she does to remain silent about her mother's lesbian relationship: 'If I told them

I think I'd be pushed out and they wouldn't want to play with me and stuff. ... I won't tell people that I think will be horrible to me about it.'

Trust becomes a key discriminating factor in how children of lesbian-headed families decide when and with whom they can be open about their family stories; and this includes being able to trust friends, their teachers and the school to respond appropriately. Schools are in a position to provide a context in which children's family stories can be told and heard in such a way as to encourage positive self-perceptions about their families in these children.

Conclusion

Primary schools have a key role in providing an environment in which children of lesbian-headed families get recognition and affirmation of their family life. Especially for the families in which there are two mothers or a mother and lesbian co-parent, getting external validation for the family and the parenting relationships is crucial in affirming the role of the non-biological co-parent. Being open to the possibilities of how family is done means not only being inclusive and thoughtful about events that provide creative opportunities like mothers' day and fathers' day but also involves being aware that children may need support from teachers and/or the school in negotiating friendships and fallouts with other children and possibly those children's parents.

Primary schools might benefit from acquiring an understanding about how lesbian parents prepare their children for going out into their own spheres of life and give them skills and strategies for dealing with others' responses to their difference as a family. An agenda for change within primary education might include acknowledgement that:

- lesbian-headed families are created in diverse ways that may or may not include fathers or non-biological co-parents

- parents prepare and skill up their children so they can take the lead in their own spheres about how they tell their family story, to whom and when

- children have different ways in which they approach the telling of their family story that can change over time

- they may or may not want individual help from teachers or their parents at various times

- children are watchful of how safe the school environment feels for telling their family story. This puts the onus on schools to live up to the expectations of these children and deliver a context in which they can tell their family stories with pride

- schools can make a difference to children feeling that their family lives are valid and that this work needs to extend beyond the curriculum to creating a whole school environment that is inclusive of these children's experiences and acts to prevent negative responses by other children and their families

This confirms that schools – who can influence the responses of not only their teachers but also the children's peers – have a key role in facilitating children feeling confident that telling their family stories will be received with respect and affirmation. The HFeS Guidance provides the framework for that to be the case. It remains to be seen how primary schools will rise to the challenge.

Note

1 For example Stonewall, the lobbying organisation for LGBQ people in the UK, launched their *Spell it out* DVD at a national conference entitled Tackling homophobia in our schools in July 2006. A keynote speaker at the conference was Jim Knight MP Minister for Schools.

References

Department for Education and Employment (2000) *Sex and Relationship Guidance.* London: Department for Education and Employment

Donovan, C and Wilson, A (2008) Integrity and imagination: exploring the narrative process of lesbian couples becoming parents. *Culture, Health and Society*

Finch, J and Mason, J (1993) *Negotiating Family Responsibilities.* London: Routledge

Gabb, J (2004) Critical differentials: querying the incongruities with research on lesbian parent families. *Sexualities* 7(2) p167-182

Gartrell, N, Hamilton, J, Banks, A, Mosbacher, D, Reed, N, Sparks, C and Bishop, H. (1996) The National Lesbian Family Study: 1. interviews with prospective mothers. *American Journal of Orthopsychiatry* 66(2) p272-281

Gartrell, N, Deck, A, Rodas, C, Peyser, H and Banks, A (2005) The National Lesbian Family Study: 4. interviews with the 10-year-old children. *American Journal of Orthopsychiatry* 75(4) p518-524

Golombok, S, Spencer, A and Rutter, M (1983) Children in lesbian and single-parent households: psychosexual and psychiatric appraisal. *Journal of Child Psychology and Psychiatry* 24(4) p551-572

Lindsay, J, Perlesz, A, Brown, R, McNair, R, de Vaus, D and Pitts, M (2006) Stigma or respect: lesbian-parented families negotiating school settings. *Sociology* 40(6) p1059-1077

Oswald, R (2002) Resilience within the family networks of lesbians and gay men: intentionality and redefinition. *Journal of Marriage and Family* 64(2) p374-383

Patterson, C (2006) Children of lesbian and gay parents. *Association for Psychological Science* 15(5) p241-244

Tasker, F (2005) Lesbian mothers, gay fathers, and their children: a review. *Developmental and Behavioural Pediatrics* 26(3) p224-240

Weeks, J, Heaphy, B and Donovan, C (2001) *Same Sex Intimacies: families of choice and other life experiments*. Routledge: London

3

School: the best days of your life?

Stephen Whittle, Lewis Turner
and Maryam Al-Alami

This chapter is an excerpt from Engendered Penalties: Transgender and Transsexual People's Experiences of Inequality and Discrimination (2007), a major research project undertaken by these authors in 2006 for the Equalities Review. They adopted a mixed quantitative and qualitative approach to collecting and analysing information on transgender and transsexual people's experiences of inequality and discrimination in the UK. In the introduction to the report, the authors caution us to remember that the three categories generally used to describe trans people – transvestite, transgender and transsexual – are simplistic; that trans people often have complex gender identities, and may move over time from one 'trans' category into another. This good advice applies to those who work with children too. The research illustrates that waiting until children are old enough to 'know for sure' may prevent schools from supporting pupils who are gender variant. The research presented here complements the stories told in this book by GLYM and Frankham and also Hinton, suggesting that questioning everyday school practices such as school uniform regulations and organisation of sport might improve children's school experience.

Transphobic harassment and bullying

This data draws upon an Online Survey of 873 self-identified trans respondents conducted during the month of August 2006. The results indicate that the majority of respondents experienced levels of transphobic bullying by their peers and members of staff at school. Respondents' comments such as the following illustrate how transphobia affected their school performance and well-being:

> Physical and mental bullying in my school was quite bad for myself (including transphobic comments) As a result I had little concentration on studies or exams and hated being in school, a few times fearing for my life.

> Constant bullying makes it difficult for anyone to learn and work.

> I found the whole of secondary education very traumatic, to the point I left as soon as I could. I returned to further and higher education later in my life.

The figures from the online survey, particularly for trans men, show higher levels of harassment and bullying than the published statistics on the school experiences of Lesbian Gay and Bisexual (LGB) children. A large scale study of lesbians, gay men, heterosexual men, heterosexual women and bisexual people found that 51 percent of gay men compared to 47 percent of heterosexual males, and 30 percent of lesbians compared to 20 percent of heterosexual women, were bullied at school (King and McKeown, 2003). But a smaller scale study of 190 LGB adults by Rivers (2001) found that the great majority (82%) had been called names at school.

The experiences of trans-identified people as reported show similar figures, except for trans men, who would have had to present as girls, though probably tomboyish girls, report far higher rates of harassment and bullying than either lesbians, heterosexual women, gay men or trans women.

Tomboys vs sissy boys

From the online results it appears that slightly more trans men were verbally abused at school and 'tomboys' had the worst time of all. When the frequency of reports was aggregated, we found that 64 percent of natal females with a male identity and 44 percent of natal males with a female identity experienced harassment or bullying at school.

Respondents were asked if they had experienced any forms of abuse at school (see Figure 6.6). They could tick more than one box to show more than one type of transphobic behaviour.

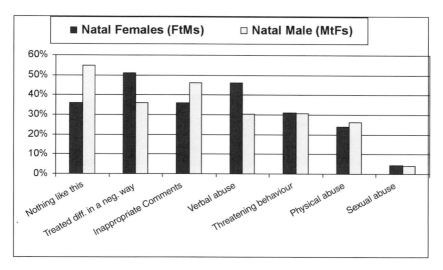

Figure 6.6: Young trans people's experiences of bullying at school by gender

Figure 6.6 shows that natal male children with female identities suffer comparably less harassment at school than natal female children with male identities. For example, over half (55%) of natal males identifying as female recorded that none of the above happened to them compared to only 36 percent of natal females identifying as males. This does not correspond with other research on the sanctions against non-gender normative behaviour of children, which claim that there is less tolerance to 'sissy boys' or effeminate boys than girls who display masculine attributes (Zucker *et al*, 1997; Martin, 1990; Fagot, 1977). But there is little if any research on the 'tomboy' at school. There is an inherent assumption that young masculine females do not face the same issues as young effeminate boys, but our research shows clearly that this is not the case.

However, even if the threshold for gender non-conformity in boys may be lower, there is evidence to suggest that boys learn to hide their cross-gender behaviour or identity – because they are aware of the peer pressure for gender conformity. Indeed, evidence suggests that under these circumstances, gender conformity is increased to avoid social rejection (Rudman and Fairchild, 2004). This process was described by several respondents who were natal males:

> I learned to live in stealth as a boy in order to survive. My schools were transphobic in that transness was not even remotely an option. (survey respondent)

> I became solitary, insular and insecure. I went to great lengths to conceal my trans characteristics. (survey respondent)

> I hid my trans status absolutely by being withdrawn and unsociable. (survey respondent)

> I never felt I fitted in. You learn very quickly to hide who you are. (survey respondent)

> I had to hide my gender issues, especially in school. My life would not have been worth living. (survey respondent)

> I kept my transgender secret. My school was a hostile environment for many people. (survey respondent)

It may be that trans men (natal females) experienced more harassment at school because their gender difference was more apparent because they could not abide wearing stereotypical girl's school uniform, and also expressing discomfort at their developing female bodies:

> As I was pressured to behave and dress as a girl, this severely affected my self esteem and my attendance to specific lessons. I felt I was not given the same treatment and help as the other children as I behaved and dressed differently.

> I was always the one picked out... because I was clearly 'queer' (I always wore the shirt and tie to school, even in summer, as I would not wear the dress, and would not wear stockings or tights) I somehow was noticed.

> In my first year I was sent to the headmaster's office and humiliated for refusing to wear a skirt. In the end I had no choice. I avoided going to school as much as I could get away with.

> Since I started presenting more masculine (eg cutting off my long hair), I have been subjected to abuse from other pupils, leading to depression. (this respondent is currently at school)

The theory that natal males may learn to hide their female identification because of peer pressure from other boys is borne out by the statistics showing who harasses trans children (see Figure 6.7). All the respondents reported being harassed more by other children than by teachers and other staff, but there is again a surprising gender

28

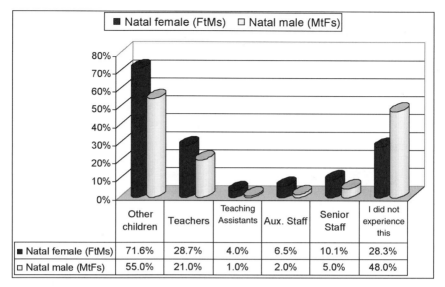

Figure 6.7: Trans children's experiences at school by gender

difference with female to male trans people reporting the most harassment by all categories of school staff and children. Over 70 percent of female to male trans men reported being bullied by other children, compared to just over 50 percent of male to female trans women. Less than a third of trans men said they did not experience bullying compared to 48 percent of trans women (see above).

The effects of transphobic bullying

Previous research on LGB experiences of bullying at school has linked it to absenteeism and truancy. Research conducted by Rivers (2000) found that 72 percent of lesbian, gay and bisexual (LGB) adults reported a regular history of absenteeism at school because of homophobic harassment. Our research also found this to be the case. Respondents were asked to describe how their experiences at school might have affected their performance at school or in exams and many described being absent from school or not completing their studies because of transphobic bullying:

> I tried to go to school as little as possible as I hated wearing a skirt and being treated like a girl.

I had to skip a lot of classes because I developed severe anxiety and was unable to cope with the pressure of constant abuse.

I did not complete my studies.

I was hardly in school due to bullying.

Bullying/isolation led to me leaving school at the earliest opportunity and avoiding any further education until [I was] 40 years old.

I was off school most the time.

I left school as soon as possible, (when I was) 15 years (old). No O-levels. [I've] had to study hard since to make up for this. (I) feared going to school, [especially] sports.

Despite the bullying a significant number of respondents in the survey are well educated, far exceeding the national norms (Figure 6.8). Many respondents stated that they returned to continue their education as adults, which may explain the high numbers of respondents educated to degree level and above, compared with the national average.

There was also a disproportionate number of respondents who left school after GSCE or equivalent Level 2 qualifications.

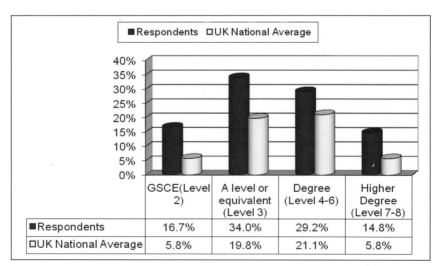

	GSCE(Level 2)	A level or equivalent (Level 3)	Degree (Level 4-6)	Higher Degree (Level 7-8)
■Respondents	16.7%	34.0%	29.2%	14.8%
□UK National Average	5.8%	19.8%	21.1%	5.8%

Figure 6.8: Educational achievements of respondents compared to national average (based on national statistics indicating the level of highest educational qualification held by people of working age in the UK in 2005)

There is a view that a reason for the overall higher educational attainment of trans people is that undertaking gender reassignment is such a complex and difficult project that those who are more highly educated may be the ones who find it easier to navigate the process. However, that fails to accommodate the bulge at the lower end of educational achievement. This group may well include individuals who could have gone on to achieve more but who instead chose to leave because of the bullying they experienced, and who have not yet returned to education.

What is clear is that many trans people are 'second chancers'. They return to education as mature students and, arguably, once they have learned that they can literally do anything, they take up the challenge and do particularly well. Nevertheless, we should also keep in mind that there may be many trans-identified people who leave school early and who do not have the life skills they need to get through the system and the stigmatisation and to make full transition as an adult.

Nowadays the FTM (female to male) Network helpline gets many calls from young ftms. One of the problems they face is that school uniform is sold, and worn, in far too gendered a way. The uniform may allow trousers, but despite our supposedly more gender-free society, children's and adolescent's clothing has nowadays lost any sense of being unisex or gender neutral and this is a problem. A boy cannot find shoes that are not trainers (which many schools will not allow) or black with thick heavy soles. Similarly, a girl who wants to dress in trousers will find they are all tapered and shaped to accentuate the hips, and the blouses to emphasise the breasts.

What is clear from the evidence is that:

- transphobic bullying is rife and there is a need for education of not only children but also school staff

- research is needed into the experience of trans-identified or masculine female adolescents and their need for protection from bullying

- projects are needed to ensure trans-identified young people are helped to stay on at school, rather than leave and seek education as 'second chancers'

■ research should explore the reasons why trans people appear so well educated as adults, and to discover whether less able trans-identified youth are ill equipped to make a full transition later in life

References

Fagot, B (1977) Consequences of moderate cross-gender behaviour in preschool children. *Child Development* 48(3) p902-907

King, M and McKeown, E (2003) *Mental health and social wellbeing of gay men, lesbians and bisexuals in England and Wales.* London: Royal Free College and University Medical School

Martin, C (1990) Attitudes and expectations about children with nontraditional and traditional gender roles. *Sex Roles* 22(3-4) p151-166

Rivers, I (2000) Social exclusion, absenteeism and sexual minority youth. *Support for Learning* 15(1) p13-17

Rivers, I (2001) The bullying of sexual minorities at school: its nature and long-term correlates. *Educational and Child Psychology* 18(1) p33-46

Rudman, L and Fairchild K (2004) Reactions to counterstereotypic behaviour: the role of backlash in cultural stereotype maintenance. *Journal of Personality and Social Psychology* 87(2) p157-176

Whittle, S, Turner, L and Al-Alami, M (2007) *Engendered Penalties: Transgender and Transsexual People's Experiences of Inequality and Discrimination.* London: The Qualities Review

Zucker, K, Bradley, S and Sanikhani, M (1997) Sex differences in referral rates of children with gender identity disorder: some hypotheses. *Journal of Abnormal Child Psychology* 25(3) p217-227

4

Walking the talk: young people making identities

Debbie Epstein and Richard Johnson

In this chapter, Epstein and Johnson explore the ways in which identities are formed in relation to institutional sites such as schools, commercial popular culture and household and family relations. These identities are developed in the context of social relations of power in terms of sexuality, gender and race. There is a tendency within any society to pathologise certain forms of identity. However, the view that versions of sexuality which are not traditionally heterosexual are some kind of condition is one which has lent itself, in the past, to practices most people would now reject as unethical. Yet even if we no longer try to cure young lesbians, gay men and bisexual people, neither do we provide appropriate and available models or advice for them. In Part Two, Vicars' chapter on the school experiences of a gay boy, Jenkins' reflections on the experiences of growing up transgender and GLYM and Frankham's memories of failing to fit into sex/gender norms poignantly illustrate what can happen when children find themselves in the process of developing pathologised identities.

Introduction

How can we understand how young people form their identities, particularly in relation to sexuality, gender and race? This question is at the heart of this chapter, which draws on work we have done together and independently over the last seventeen years, when we first began working on sexuality issues.

In this chapter, we draw on a number of examples taken from fieldwork over several years and in different projects in order to explore the formation of young people's sexual identities. We argue that young people produce themselves as raced, gendered and sexualised actors in and through certain key relationships. Their most immediate contexts are the sexual cultures of young people themselves, formed in relation to institutional sites such as schools, commercial popular culture and household and family relations. We suggest that identities are power-fully formed through what Connell (1995) has called 'body-reflexive practices' – that is, the circuit of effects between bodily experiences, emotional life and the cultural explanations given for them. But impor-tantly, these experiences and understandings are developed in the con-text of social relations of power. Sexual differences, for example, are always accompanied and mutually shaped by other differences that make a difference in people's everyday lives (such as race, gender or embodiment). Immediate, face-to-face interactions are always imbued with larger cultural formations around the sexual, which are repro-duced and sometimes changed in such practices as media representa-tion, political and legal processes, the sale and consumption of com-modities, education and scientific, professional and expert knowledges. We suggest that these understandings have implications for profes-sional practices for they indicate that practitioners in, for instance, caring, teaching or medical professions are directly and actively in-volved in the identity construction of their young clients, students or patients in the same moment as they construct their own professional identities. We finish by arguing that ethical practice with young people in relation to their emergent sexual identities is only achievable when professionals are self-reflective about the limitations of their own hori-zons and aware of their partiality.

Six young people in search of identities

This section introduces the six young people we have chosen from Debbie's fieldwork as exemplars of the complex processes of identity work and formation in which all the young people we have worked with over the years have been involved. These are young people whose identities are, in different ways, under pressure and therefore show up more clearly the negotiations, limitations and agentic performances in which they are involved.

1) Tracy

Tracy was a young White working-class woman at a large comprehensive single-sex state school in the West Midlands. She had a somewhat unhappy relationship to schooling and was in one of the lower streams of Year 10 (14/15 years old). She often missed school, apparently truanting with parental consent. She was the subject of much interest and gossip amongst both teachers and students because she presented herself as interested in and knowledgeable about sex and as sexually active. She talked about her relationships with young (and older) men, carried a condom and displayed it with a flourish in sex education lessons. She persisted in wearing make-up on the days she did come to school, despite repeated prohibition. Teachers (and maybe health professionals) perceived her as being at risk of an early pregnancy. In discussions with me, Tracy expressed simultaneous pleasure and discomfort with her public image and reputation. She gave the impression that she was a good deal less sexually active and experienced than her reputation or self-presentation as a highly hetero-sexualised version of the feminine would suggest. She produced a performative femininity in which the different aspects of her social identity (classed, raced, gendered and sexualised) all played their part. It is a version of heterosexual young woman which has been subject to savage satire on UK television's comedy programme, *Little Britain*.

2) Simon

Simon was a young middle-class White gay man in a grammar (selective) school in London. He was tall and well-built and athletic and was the captain of the rugby team. He had a boyfriend at the same school who was also in the team and they went around together, often holding hands and, in his own words, 'completely out'. Neither he nor his boyfriend, Peter, experienced homophobic bullying but they knew that this was only because of their obvious size, athleticism and, as Simon pointed out, assumed heterosexuality. In other words, he and Peter were completely 'out' but nobody saw that they were anything other than 'good friends'. He was aware that there was a danger of becoming the subject of homophobia and one of his avoidance strategies was to take part in bullying of more effete and feminised young men in the school. Simon's self-presentation was as ultra-masculine, confident, well-groomed and smooth. His size and evident athleticism confirmed both his masculinity and his assumed heterosexuality. He had much social capital gained from his class, the school he attended and his educational and sporting success. This was virtually a text-book version of hegemonic masculinity – the masculinity assumed to be desirable – except that he was gay.

3) Elias and Levi

Elias was a working-class Turkish-origin boy, just pre-teen. He was highly attractive, both in his personality and looks. He was the most popular boy in the year group among both boys and girls in his London school. But he could be quite troublesome (and therefore less attractive) to teachers and had difficulty maintaining an acceptable standard in his schoolwork. He spent most of his time with his best friend, Levi, an equally attractive young African-Caribbean boy. Both were much in demand as boyfriends and knew themselves to be so. They already took their heterosexual attractiveness for granted, but were emotionally more involved with each other (and with Arsenal, their local football club, which plays in the Premier League and has an international reputation) than with any of their putative girlfriends, with whom they spent little time. He and Levi were occasionally involved in sexually harassing the very girls who fancied them. The girls seemed to find this at once exasperating, threatening and exciting. In some ways it added to the attractiveness of the boys rather than detracting from it, although the girls also reported finding the boys' invasions of their changing rooms during swimming quite distressing. The versions of masculinity presented by these boys were very much nuanced by ethnicity in style of dress, embodiment and behaviour. Levi, for example, obviously spent many hours having his head shaved with precisely the right patterns, and walked with the kind of swagger that is often adopted by older African-Caribbean young men in London. Elias' self-presentation was somewhat less swaggering but, like his friend, he could certainly walk the desirable walk.

4) Morgan

Morgan was a middle-class White girl in a mixed school who chose this pseudonym from the feminist version of the Arthurian legend, naming herself for Morgan le Fey, the wicked sister in mainstream versions, but on the side of the good old mother religions in some feminist versions.

She was in her early teens, and was the most popular girl in her year, especially amongst the girls. She had had a boyfriend, Michael, since Year 5 (9-10 years old) – her 'childhood sweetheart'. She was very much in charge of all her relationships. When she was a young child in primary school, I had observed how she was already leading the other children, boys and girls, in play that was both familial and sexualised in the broadest sense. She and Michael were the lead characters in an imaginative narrative game, which continued from day to day over several weeks. Rather like a soap opera, a familiar genre for the children, each playtime produced a new episode. These always involved the mother (Morgan) and father (Michael) of the family and assorted offspring, played by their closest friends. Different episodes might include doctors, social workers, teachers or other members of the community with whom this fictional family came into contact. Morgan was very good at football, which she began to play at primary school in conditions that encouraged girls to play it (see Epstein *et al*, 2001) and this was the source of some of her popularity. She was also invested in a version of girl power derived from the Spice Girls when they were popular, but taken beyond them in her everyday life in school. She was assertive and a high achiever, and had good relationships with adults as well as children.

5) Lara

Lara was of Panjabi origin and identified as a lesbian. She had done so since her mid-teens, and at that time believed herself to be the only Asian lesbian in the world. This was her own description:

> I thought I was the only Asian lesbian in the world. I was *the* Asian lesbian and I was put on earth to sort of start this revolution amongst Asian lesbians, for, about being gay. And that was my purpose in life. ... And, like, y'know, my image of lesbianism was like this short-haired, really butch White dyke, bovver boots style, and here was me, this little Punjabi woman, this Punjabi girl who, y'know, loved long earrings and long hair .... used to love Asian clothes.

Lara's self-presentation was very much embedded in both her gender and ethnicity. Her self-descriptive words show how important both were to her.

Identity as self-production/agency

We suggest that young people produce themselves as gendered, sexua-lised and racialised actors in and through certain key relationships. Their most immediate contexts are the cultures of young people them-selves, formed in relation to institutional sites such as schools, com-mercial popular culture and household and family relations. In this context, it makes sense to think of questions of the health, well-being and self-image of young people as being entwined with questions of identity and the care and production of the self. We understand identity here not as something given by anatomy or genes or even psychosocial development, but as something that is produced, by hard work and active performance. It is constructed at many different levels. Both the inter- and intra-personal play their part as the constant reiterations of performative practices that, as Judith Butler (1990; 1993) suggests, come to be written on the body. These iterative performances are never exactly the same as each other, and are relational in kind. They can be seen as key in the production of self. Of course this self-production occurs in conditions that young people do not control. They are not the free creators of the capacities and limits of their bodies. They do not usually invent altogether anew the stories with which they narrate their lives. They do not produce the commodities they use to make up a style. They are emerging from the relative powerlessness of childhood into an already unequally structured adult world. But they do not passively receive the imprint of their cultural and social environment. They are not simple receptors of useful information or rational adult advice.

We take it as axiomatic that making one's self, one's identity, involves one's relations with others. It is about not only who one wants to be, who one wants to be with, who one wants to be like, who one wants to be liked by, but also who one wants to be different from, who one dis-likes, who makes one gag, who is one's Other. Both sides of the love/hate, desire/repulsion divides are important in this context. The mak-ing of identity is both an intra- and interpersonal process in which who one is (becoming) derives from a combination of how one sees one's self, one's personal histories and one's relations with and to others. Here we are talking about all kinds of significant others in a person's life. Parents, siblings and early experience of being cared for, or not, are im-portant here but are not the exclusive source of identity making. Other people are also involved, whether they are mates, friends, enemies, lovers, idols or hate figures; models and anti-models. In the school context such others are likely to be other pupils or teachers, while beyond that there are more distant figures like pop stars and celebrities, whose place in the imagination is the result of a negotiation between the work such people do to construct their own images and the multiplicity of ways in which they are read. Identity making is relational, both at the level of fantasy and in everyday interactions with others including, importantly, one's peer groups.

Our exemplary characters illustrate many of the practices through which young people produce themselves. As shown elsewhere (Epstein *et al*, 2001), the pleasurable repetitions of play by Morgan, her boyfriend Michael and their friends in imaginative games involved not only domestic characters – mummies, daddies and babies – but also social workers and doctors. Simon and Peter produced themselves in a different kind of play – rugby – that was recognised and regulated by rules of team sport and cultural codes of masculinity. The constitution of a personal style was already well in train by Elias and Levi, who certainly dressed the dress, walked the walk and talked the talk of the older young men they admired, while Tracy's heterosexual explicitness involved make-up and dress, particularly the adaptation of school uniform to make it sexy. Lara, on the other hand, was struggling to find a style, not happy either in the butch dyke image of Whiteness she perceived as lesbian, or as a conventional heterosexual Asian woman – notwithstanding her liking for girlie/traditional dress. She had to make herself up as unique as she went along – the only Asian lesbian in the world.

There are two important qualifications of this argument so far. First, although we do often find ourselves admiring the resourcefulness of young people, we do not want to present a simple and heroic view of their self-production. The processes of identity formation are full of ambivalence and contradiction. One of Tracy's strategies, for example, was to import a knowing adult sexuality into the officially desexualised context of the school. She understood that this gave her a certain status, even prominence, but she also paid a heavy reputational price for her bad girl image, as we discussed in *Schooling Sexualities* (Epstein and Johnson, 1998). We question whether this was an identity strategy that could be happily sustained and which would help Tracy develop a sense of satisfaction and well-being in her life. In enacting the 'bad' or 'sexy' girl, Tracy may have been defending herself against anxiety-producing situations. Was she, for example, being brash, difficult and rejecting of school values in order to save herself from being rejected? Asking such questions about young people's moves in relation to school or family situations may not lead to answers, but might cause teachers to give pause to their irritation and anger. Second, we are far from arguing that young people's agency always produces good outcomes for themselves and others. It is clear, for instance, that the strategies pursued by Tracy, Elias and Levi may deliver them to particular subordinated class destinations as academically failing girl and boys. Levi, particularly, as an African-Caribbean boy seemed likely to attract the racist attentions of the police in his middle and later teens – and both he and Elias seemed quite likely to end up on the wrong side of the law. Furthermore, these boys could be a problem for the girls, with their harassing invasions of the swimming pool changing rooms, for example.

Body-reflexive practices

In arguing that young people produce themselves in cultural ways, we are not suggesting that the body, as in some sense given, is not important. Connell (1995) uses the term 'body reflexive practices' to explain how people have material, bodily experiences but the only way in which they can make sense of them is through their cultural understandings. We conceptualise this as a kind of embodied 'circuit of culture' (Johnson, 1986) in which such experiences:

> [go] from bodily interaction and bodily experience, via socially structured bodily fantasy ... to the construction of fresh ... relationships centring on new bodily interactions. This is not simply a matter of social meanings or categories being imposed ... The body-reflexive practice calls them into play, while the bodily experience ... energizes the circuit. (Connell, 1995, p62)

If we take the case of Simon and his boyfriend, Peter, and start with bodily experiences, we note that they were active lovers as schoolboys. Their experience both of playing rugby for the school and of homosexual practices were understood and interpreted by them through cultural means. They shared particular versions of bodily pleasure – in sex and in physical fitness – producing themselves as desired and desirable in particular ways. They worked on their bodies, which were given as large and with a talent for sport, to produce themselves as athletic, strong and skilful in particular ways for the successful playing of rugby. But for that to happen there had to be practices socially available, in their case, the game of rugby, that provided points of recognition for big, strong gay boys – in a sporting culture which is infamously homophobic, misogynist and, at the same time, homoerotic. And so we come back to the body again. The boys had the big bodies required for success in rugby, and perhaps the innate tendency towards good bodily coordination, but they developed these capacities through practice and training and this involved work on their bodies and on their embodied identities.

If we take the example of Tracy's potential and predicted teenage pregnancy, we can see that this would be a very active transformation, and creation, of the body. While teachers, health professionals and policy-makers may see the disadvantages to teenage pregnancies for both mothers and children – the interruption to education, the risk of poverty, for instance – it is important to recognise that pregnancy can be, and often is, a strategy with its own rationality – one which wins the girl adulthood and emotional relationship, as well as work, worry, expense and damage to her education (Bullen *et al*, 2000; Alldred and David, 2007). This is why the idea, which is popular amongst policy-makers and some educators in the UK, of giving young women or men a doll which cries and needs feeding in order to discourage them from becoming pregnant or impregnating someone is a chimera. Winnicott (1965) named the intense preoccupation that mothers usually have with their new babies 'primary maternal preoccupation'. He says that:

> the point is that towards the end of the pregnancy and for a few weeks after the birth of a child the mother is preoccupied with (or better, 'given over to') the care of her baby, which at first seems like part of herself; moreover she is very much identified with the baby and knows quite well what the baby is feeling like. For this she uses her own experiences as a baby. In this way the mother is herself in a dependent state and vulnerable. (Winnicott, 1965, p85)

However, young women have neither the biological imperative of pregnancy, birth and accompanying hormones, nor the emotional connection to these dolls. Dolls do not return love, depend on the mother, respond emotionally, smile, hug, grasp and all the other things a baby does to engage the mother and other adults in its own infantile production of itself, not to mention the response the mother has to the baby. The doll, however realistic it is made to seem, provides nothing on our body reflexive circuit to engage young women; the embodied experience, the cultural expectation and the psychic and emotional investments made by most women in their children are all absent.

Contexts, social conditions

When young people give meaning to their lives, they use narratives and images that have already been produced elsewhere. For example, Morgan's choice of her pseudonym drew on the feminist version, told her by her mother, of the Arthurian legend. Equally, Elias' name and something of his reputation appeared in the repeated insertion of it into traditional skipping and clapping rhymes performed in the playground by girls in his and other classes. Lara, on the other hand, used and enjoyed traditional dress, while not wanting to occupy the traditional female position within her culture. One way of understanding the roles of those who work with young people as practitioners and knowledge producers is that they/we operate as another source of cultural narratives and identities for young people. This operates across the gamut of public professions. Valerie Harwood (2006) discusses how the label 'conduct disorder', for example, affects the ways in which young people so diagnosed see themselves. She suggests that psychiatry, as a form of knowledge and a practice, puts pressure on clients to produce themselves as psychiatric subjects, that is, as mentally disordered. Similarly, teachers and professionals working with young people are necessarily involved in the process of their identity production in ways that are backed by particular forms of power, from academic assessment to psychiatric sectioning. We can broaden the picture here, and insist that young people make themselves with socially recognised identities already current in the larger culture. There is always an individual appropriation, a biographical inflection, but the work of identity is always doubly pressured: first, from the level of material and bodily resources; second from the most insistent or dominant story lines. In sexual relations, for example, the presumption of heterosexuality always makes it more difficult for young gay men and lesbians to seek appropriate advice on sexual and other matters.

In Figure 1, we present as a diagram what we have called a circuit of identity production. Embodiment is part of this larger picture, but only a part of it. At each point in this circuit we can identify a range of power relations and inequalities in relation to the resources, possibilities of recognition and the sustainability of strategies of identity available to people in different social positions. If we start at the top of the diagram, it is possible to identify those identities that are most readily recognised socially – and these vary with time and location. The introduction of the institution of civil partnerships in the UK may well have the effect of making non-heterosexual relationships more easily recognisable as socially acceptable. However, just as legislation making racial discrimination unlawful does not end racism, this does not mean that it is socially acceptable in schools for young people to identify themselves as, in some way, queer. Rather, the heterosexual economy of schools (Hey, 1997) is such that the presumption of heterosexuality continues to

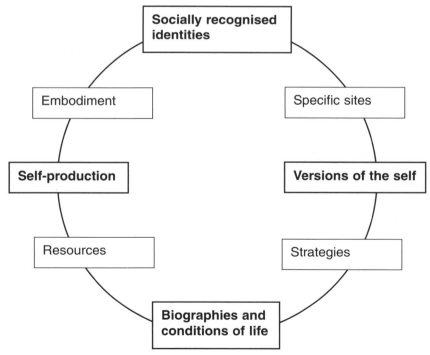

Figure 1: Circuit of identity production

be strong and it may be very difficult for young people, especially boys, to hold on to such identities with any conviction, safety or self- esteem.

Similarly, O'Flynn and Epstein (2005) have shown how little social recognition is available to refugee students in the UK who have non-normatively heterosexual families. Such students have difficulty in coming out about their familial organisation at school to the other students or to the official school, for example, in how their next-of-kin is named when marriage is polygamous. Eve Sedgwick (1990) has argued that the metaphor of the closet is the metaphor of the age – that we all know that the 'closet' exists and that it plays as large a part in the production and propping up of heterosexuality as it does in the secreting of homosexuality, and Sarah O'Flynn's (2007) work demonstrates this admirably. If we then move round the circuit through specific sites and strategies to versions of the self which young people may hold, develop, nurture or reject and their personal biographies and conditions of life – what the realms of possibility are for them in the processes of self-production and contexts of power relations within which they take place – we can see that each point on the circuit holds different complications and potential difficulties.

It is impossible in this context to separate gender from sexuality or vice versa in any sensible way. Gender is performed through sexuality and sexuality through gender. Equally, in class-organised and racialised societies, race and ethnicity are always also gendered, sexualised and classed – hence the importance of noting not only the gender of our exemplary characters but also their race, sexuality and class. One does not exist without the other and each is performed through the other (see also Nayak, 1999).

One more point before turning to some practical implications of this analysis. Because of the close relation between growing up, in this cultural sense, and the larger cultural field, contradictions in the field press particularly hard upon young people. Sexuality is a good example. As we are all aware, there are marked tendencies towards crisis in the most approved forms of intimate and sexual relations, especially the institution of marriage and in the most familiar forms of gender relations. One of the ways crisis has been handled in the last twenty or thirty years is to insist on marriage as a centrepiece for sex education, a practice which has been increasingly closely regulated – and this is certainly the case in the UK government's *Sex and Relationship Education Guidance* (DfEE, 2000). Teachers and children are often blamed for a much larger social movement which has produced and continues to produce an enormous diversity of ways of sexual living, which have their own legitimacy.

At the same time, as Haskey (1998: 32-33) notes, people in the UK are living in more varied kinds of family than ever before. For example, the *General Household Survey 1991* reported that while just over two thirds of children under the age of 16 were living with two biological parents, not all of them were married. Furthermore, in the ten years between 1981 and 1991 the proportion of children living in lone (mother) families increased from 8 percent to 17 percent for under 4s, from 9 percent to 19 percent for 5 to 9-year olds and increased by 50 percent for 10 to 15-year olds (OPCS, 1993). This is an on-going trend, and Gingerbread, a charity supporting single parents, estimated that between a third and half of the next generation will spend some time in lone parent families (Gingerbread, 1998). The number of children of these ages who are step-parented has also increased dramatically in the period, with a high ratio of remarriage following divorce (Newman and Smith, 1997). The Social Exclusion Unit's report on *Teenage Pregnancy* (SEU, 1999) reported that 56,000 young women under the age of 20 (out of 90,000 conceptions) give birth in the UK each year, including 8,000 under the age of 16. As this report shows, these young women are likely to live with their children in single-parent families or multigenerational families, but are less likely to live with their partner and child or in a legal marriage. The incidence of divorce and remarriage means that many other children are living in families with complicated patterns of step-parenting, step-siblings and spending time with each parent in different households. Equally, the growth in the prevalence of same-sex parenting means that there are young people in many schools who, while identifying heterosexual themselves, have lesbian or gay parents. Consequently, it makes no sense to educate children as if monogamous, heterosexual partnership were still the only socially approved form of sexual life. They know this not to be the case from their own experiences and those of their friends.

Conclusion: implications for practice

As we come to the end of our argument, we want to stress the absolute importance of taking account of what might be called the identity projects of the people with whom teachers and other professionals deal. This does not mean just trying to understand or empathise with them, but making critical yet respectful evaluations of the particular projects of those with whom we are dealing. If we look at the examples we gave above, we can ask some questions about our young people.

Elias and Levi, for example, are 'failing boys', so where will they go for employment, to sustain their lifestyle as potentially good-looking young men with expensive tastes in consumer goods and no means of economic support? For teachers, the practical endeavour must be to work with them to develop their own projects in ways that are more sustainable, less damaging and ultimately probably happier. For health practitioners, there will be other, related concerns – for example around questions of alcohol and boy-on-boy violence. Similarly, as we pointed out above, the possibility that Tracy will become a young single mother has implications for her health and education. But to approach her in ways that confirm her childishness, which she is trying to leave behind her, is neither respectful nor helpful. Consequently, teachers need to be aware of how their practices construct possibilities and spaces for young people's identity production in school contexts and, in this context, of how their own practice constructs identity in relation to the sexual. There is a tendency within any society to pathologise certain forms of identity. However, the view that versions of sexuality which are not traditionally heterosexual are some kind of condition is one which has lent itself in the past to practices most people would now reject as unethical, like trying to cure homosexuality. But even if we don't, now, try to cure young lesbians, gay men and bisexual people, neither do we give them appropriate and available models or advice, medical or social or educational.

Finally, some points about knowledge, including the status of our own knowledges as practitioners and researchers and that of teachers and other professionals. We follow much contemporary debate in the human and social sciences in doubting the possibility of an objective, god-like stance as knowledge producers. Rather, partiality is all we have. All knowledge is produced from particular social positions in relation to the others whom we seek to know. All knowledge works with particular paradigms with their own insights, limits and closures. Scientific knowledge is only one way of knowing, but it aims at a kind of mastery which constructs the other as an object. This is so much the dominant paradigm of knowledge that it often disqualifies other ways of knowing. In fact, the approaches and methods of an enquiry are always dependent on what we want to know. If we are concerned with the cultures and identities of young people, we have to treat them as subjects and not objects, qualifying our own prejudices and power by dialogue and careful listening and watching. This model of knowledge as interpretation and understanding that attempts to cross major social differences has to make its way in a culture where young people are characteristically not listened to and are treated as the sources of problems and dangers, as victims or threats, as bearers of pathologies of different kinds. One of the aims of this chapter is to try out the affinities between our kind of understanding of young people and the practical ethical ways of relating to them which take account of our view of knowledge as partial. In thinking about the young people who have peopled our research over a long period, we end by recognising both their resourcefulness and the constraints under which they operate and in which their identities are (per)formed.

References

Alldred, P and David, M (2007) *Get Real about Sex: the politics and practice of sex education.* Maidenhead: Open University Press

Bullen, E, Kenway, J and Hey, V (2000) New Labour, social exclusion and educational risk management: the case of 'gymslip mums'. *British Educational Research Journal* 26(4) p441 – 456

Butler, J (1990) *Gender Trouble: feminism and the subversion of identity.* London: Routledge

Butler, J (1993) *Bodies that Matter: on the discursive limits of 'sex'.* London: Routledge

Connell, R.W. (1995) *Masculinities.* Cambridge, Polity

Department for Education and Employment (2000) *Sex and Relationship Guidance.* London: Department for Education and Employment

Epstein, D and Johnson, R (1998) *Schooling Sexualities.* Buckingham: Open University Press

Epstein, D, Kehily, M, Mac an Ghaill, M and Redman, P (2001) Girls and boys come out to play: making masculinities and femininities in primary playgrounds. *Men and Masculinities. Disciplining and Punishing Masculinities* 4(2) p158-72

Gingerbread (1998) *Lone Parent Families: action facts.* London: Gingerbread

Harwood, V (2006) *Diagnosing Disorderly Children: a critique of behaviour disorder discourses.* Abingdon: Routledge

Haskey, J (1998) Families: their historical context, and recent trends in the factors influencing their formation and dissolution. In David, M (ed.) *The Fragmenting Family: Does it Matter?* London: Institute of Economic Affairs

Hey, V (1997) *The Company She Keeps: an ethnography of girls' friendships.* Buckingham: Open University Press

Johnson, R (1986) What is cultural studies anyway? *Social Text* 16, p38-80

Nayak, A (1999), White English ethnicities: racism, anti-racism and student perspectives. *Race Ethnicity and Education* 2(2) p177-202

Newman, P and Smith, A (1997) *Social Focus on Families.* London: The Stationery Office

O'Flynn, S (2007) Testing times: the construction of girls' desires through secondary education. Unpublished PhD thesis, School of Social Sciences, Cardiff University.

O'Flynn, S and Epstein, D (2005) Standardising sexuality: embodied knowledge, 'Achievement' and 'Standards'. *Social Semiotics* 15(2) p183-208

OPCS (1993) *General Household Survey 1991.* London: Office for Population and Census Statistics

Sedgwick, E (1990) *Epistemology of the Closet.* Berkeley: University of California Press

SEU (1999) *Teenage Pregnancy.* London: Social Exclusion Unit

Winnicott, D (1965) From dependence towards independence in the development of the individual. In Winnicott, D (ed) *The Maturational Processes and the Facilitating Environment.* London: Karnac Books

PART TWO
Memories of transgressive childhoods

5

A pink rabbit and a blue rabbit: learning about gender (and sex) at primary school

*Lesbian and Gay Youth Manchester
and Jo Frankham*

At the Invisible Boundaries seminar in Manchester, Lesbian and Gay Youth Manchester (LGYM) delivered a performance that incorporated the text of their own childhood recollections with illustrations and artefacts. This chapter is an adaptation of that creative performance. Together with Jo Frankam, these young people explored their own memories and experiences of transgressive childhoods. In this chapter they explore some of the ways in which knowledge about same-sex attraction is explicitly withheld from children while at the same time implicit gender and behaviour norms provide negative connotations. Following on from Epstein and Johnson, this chapter illustrates how schools and other institutions in children's lives can unconsciously contribute to their construction of pathologised identities.

Introduction

This chapter was developed from a series of group discussions between members of Lesbian and Gay Youth Manchester and Jo Frankham of Manchester University. Lesbian and Gay Youth Manchester meet weekly, with the support of youth workers. The group provides a safe space for young people to meet each other and enjoy different activities together. For further information visit the website http://www.lgym. org.uk.

The discussions ranged across the themes that are raised here. When we began to talk, the consensus was that children are shielded from information about same-sex attraction and therefore do not begin to learn about it until they are in their teens. However, as we talked more it was obvious that many lessons about same-sex attraction, mostly indirect and with negative connotations, had been learned at primary school. Many of these lessons are contained within norms that are laid down about gender and what is regarded as appropriate behaviour for girls or boys.

Boys who played in the kitchen! Gender divisions in toys, games and clothing

Speaker 1 Oh my goodness – boys that played in the kitchen! Get out of my kitchen, boy! That's what it was like. Like what was a boy doing in the kitchen?! And it was really weird because the girls either wanted them to go away or mothered them.

Speaker 2 And other boys were like, 'Why is he playing in the kitchen, why isn't he playing in the sand?' Or the boys would play on the work bench with the tools and the girls had to play with the water stuff, or they could go and play in the shop.

Speaker 3 I used to sit in this little patch of mud in the playground and dig with a stick to find Australia. The teacher talked to my parents about it – she asked them to come in. And she said she was worried because I wasn't talking to people and mixing with them. I can remember my Mum talking to me about it when we got home and saying amongst other things, 'You know it's not very ladylike to sit in the mud. And dig.'

Speaker 4 Once a week we could bring toys in and some of the girls brought in this phone – it was called a 'Love Phone' and it talked. It had things on it, like, 'What's your boyfriend's name?' 'Who do you love?' And I just wasn't interested. I had my teddies and that was what I wanted and it was like – you're a baby – this is what girls should be playing with now.

Speaker 5 I saw a catalogue the other day which had a doll in it – as a stripper – and she had a pole, and a garter and fake dollar bills to pay her with. I was just shocked to see this – we didn't have anything like that when we were that age. But then it fits with what my little sister wears now – with a thong right up her middle – and playboy clothes and their jeans hanging off them. I've even seen a bunny girl outfit for a child.

Speaker 6 We had to put in a petition for the girls to be allowed to wear trousers. I put it up – and then it took about four years to go through. Then they gave us these trousers that no-one would wear because they had massive hips and tiny skinny ankles.

A pink rabbit and a blue rabbit: Learning about sex

Speaker 1 At some point in primary school there was a conversation, Did you know that some girls like girls and some boys like boys? And we were like talking about it, and I remember it really distinctly, because I said 'I don't see what's wrong with that'. And everyone looked at me – shocked – I think we must have been a bit older than 8 – like about 10? I remember thinking I don't know what they're on about – why was that

weird? It was in the same conversation that they were talking about vibrators. That was really fascinating.

Speaker 2 That was when I heard about condoms. I knew about the female pill, so I thought, 'I know what a condom is, it's a pill that the man takes'. Then later, I thought, I know what it is – it's like the thing that you put on the end of a baby's bottle ... We were all trying to find things out and trying to work it out.

Speaker 3 We used to phone sex lines and ask stupid questions like what's a blow job and stuff like that and do funny accents. But then, once, I went to the phone box on my own and I made up this story to the guy. I said that me and my female friend were caught kissing, and we weren't allowed to see each other any more and what should I do?

It was completely made up, but I think I was just testing the water. He asked me how old I was and I said, 10 or 11, whatever I was, and he said, 'You're too young, you can't ring this service'. It was like a sex line thing – it was supposed to be – for questions. It was free and it was experts about sexual health. But you would think if it's sexual health it should be sexuality as well – it's an information line.

Speaker 4 It's quite evident how primary school influences you. I can remember when I was about five and I was sat in a supermarket trolley. I saw two men shopping together and not having seen that before I asked my dad, 'How come men don't marry men and women don't marry women?' And my dad's reply was, 'Well, sometimes they do'. And that sort of satisfied my curiosity.

But then I can remember being 11 and by that time I knew definitely that that was 'wrong'. By then I'd started senior school and it was wrong to be with someone of the same sex. I became quite homophobic. Obviously something had gone on in those few years to make me think like that – to make me change my mind.

Speaker 5 I learnt all about sex from a CD-ROM. You had all these diagrams of how the body works and a cross section of the penis and vagina and little arrows for the sperm coming out. In one of our books we did have a picture of the body of a man and woman but then they still put 'the bits' in cross section. Still it was better than the other school I went to – there it was rabbits – a woman rabbit and a man rabbit – and they were in pink and blue!

Why can't I run with the lads? The gendering of sport

Speaker 1 I used to get told off for playing football when I was about 9. I'd play with the older boys and Mum would complain about me. She didn't like my shoes being scuffed, so I used to go into the toilet and clean them up.

I'd wipe my shoes off so my Mum didn't know I was playing football because it was absolutely wrong as far as she was concerned – I was not allowed to play football at school.

Some of the teachers were OK and there were three girls who wanted to play. But it was hard to get the lads to actually let you play. And when we were allowed to play, it was, 'Oh all right, but you've got to stand there then.' Eventually they had a girls' football team but I wasn't allowed to play because of my Mum. I played one game without her knowing – and I was put in goal. She found out and I was grounded. My Mum was blaming the school and it all went major up, because they'd actually arranged for a girls' football team.

Speaker 2 In our school there was actually a policy that girls weren't allowed to play football. They said they were worried that the girls would get hurt. We would actually get a detention if they found we had been playing football. The lads were quite happy to let us play but we weren't supposed to play any games with the boys – football or basketball. They had supervisors walking around and if any of the girls were caught you would get in real trouble for it.

Speaker 3 I went to an all-girls' school and we weren't allowed to play football either. It was hockey or it was netball and you had to wear a skirt. It took us two or three years before we were allowed to wear shorts. I used to get detentions for it every week because I used to refuse point blank to wear a skirt. I'd get a detention for it every week.

Speaker 4 In primary school, because of the football thing, I got all my friends together and we picketed the boys' games lesson. I just thought we'd all sit across the path so the boys couldn't get through because we wanted to play football. And a bunch of us went down and sat on this path and the boys all came out. They just walked round us but then the headteacher came out and all my friends scurried off. I just sat there on the grass on my own and it was, 'What's all this?' And I said, 'We want to play football.' And it was, 'Get back to your games lesson – now.'

Speaker 5 Why is it on sports day that the boys and the girls are segregated? Why can't the girls run with the boys? Some boys aren't very fast and some girls are.

I got to Year 6 and I only had two girls to race against because none of the other girls would do it any more. Why can't I run with the lads? But they wouldn't let me. Why can't we all just compete against each other?

Speaker 6 But what if girls were allowed to compete against the boys in Year 6 and what if they beat them?! My cousin is 5. And the other day he sat on my knee and we were just chatting. Then he looked at me funny and I said, 'What's wrong?' And he said, 'Are you a boy?' And I said, 'Is that because I've got short hair?' And he said, 'Yeah'. He's already worked out what he thinks a girl should look like and what a boy should look like and he hasn't even started primary school yet.

6

Straddling the scalpel of identity, my earliest memory

Claire Jenkins

Jenkins provides us with a personal perspective on what it might be like to realise your gendered understanding of yourself is not shared by your family, your community and even your nation(s). Through rich description and gentle irony she illustrates the ways in which a key aspect of her identity (sex: boy) was established for her from birth through the simple act of filling out mandatory bureaucratic paperwork. As a young child, Jenkins soon discovered that this simple act of registration did not coincide with her lived reality. The sounds, smells and sensations of her childhood told her a very different story of herself. She recalls the legal and social struggles of re-aligning her identities as an adult. Jenkins prepares us for Hinton's story of how parents and school staff might work together with children to support trans identities, while Stewart provides an understanding of how school can open spaces for children to express a wider spectrum of gender identities.

Pursuant to the Births and Deaths Registration Acts 1836 to 1929 I was entry number 127, born on the 1st of May 1949 at Llwynypia Hospital and given the name of Thomas Jenkins. Sex is boy. The name and surname of father is Douglas Jenkins and the name and maiden surname of mother is Thelma Parry Jenkins, formerly Parry. The rank or profession of father is General Labourer of 225 High Street Treorchy. The informant was mother T P Jenkins of 225 High Street, Treorchy and the registration took place on 18th of May 1949, the registrar being S Rees.

This is an historical fact bestowed upon me by the state, immutable and not to be changed. My life has been a struggle with the cultural, biological and legal implications of my entry of birth. I clearly remember my first encounter with this reality of history.

I was with my mam and her friend Jean in Jean's living room. In those days nearly everyone lived in terraced miners' cottages, which were built like long rows of giant caterpillars straddling the mountainsides above the valley. These cottages were built of local stone and had two bedrooms on the first floor and two rooms on the ground floor. Usually one of these ground floor rooms was the best room, which was rarely used except on very special occasions, and the other had a dual role as a living room and kitchen where the family lived. The toilet was a separate little house (*ty bach* in Welsh) at the bottom of the garden. The living room had a black leaded open fire grate on which all the cooking was done and the water boiled.

The room was full of things. Jean was untidy. I seem to remember it being warm, steamy and cosy; whether this was high humidity from the rain or condensation from the cooking I can't remember. Phyllis, Jean's daughter, was not there for some reason. I liked Phyllis because she was a girl aged about 4, my own age at that time. Anyway, Jean had bought an apron as a birthday present for her daughter. It was pretty, with flowers, two ties and a bib just like those the women wore to do their housework. Mam and Jean decided between them that I was the same size as Phyllis so they would try this apron on me to see if it would fit. So there I was. That's it really, a memory that has remained with me all my life, even though Jean, my mam and Phyllis are all Certified Copies of an Entry of Death, pursuant to the Births and Deaths Registration Act 1953.

It felt good, warm and it was right, this experience, but I remember also feeling embarrassment and shame and my body gave this away by blushing uncontrollably. This confusion convinced me that I was alone with my secret feelings. My secret feelings were wanting to be like Phyllis and dress like Phyllis whilst being with my mam and Jean in a warm safe environment. The warmth seemed the warmth of rightness and properness. Sex: boy.

Llwynypia, and *Treorci* (Treorchy) were villages but in reality were two of the connected segments making up the Rhondda valley. The

Rhondda was a communist socialist stronghold of a rigidly gendered, working class, white and yet slightly cosmopolitan community. I can remember there were two strange men: Patty who seemed to like boys and Willie who ran the boys' club. We all were in this experience a mixture of many chapels and pubs with aliens; the Chinese laundry and the small Irish-Italian Catholic Church in *Treorci*. 225 High Street was where my mam, my dad and me lived in the house of my long-widowed maternal grandmother. Gran was a formidable woman disabled by arthritis who was an active member of the Communist Party. She ran the whole family like a totalitarian state, even her sons who had long since emigrated to England to find work in the Midlands. But I saw her as understanding my secret feelings; she loved me. Sex: boy.

I wanted to be like Phyllis but that was not what the hospital had said; I was a boy. I had even by the time of this early memory learned that I must perform like a boy or risk ending up like Patty: constantly teased, bullied and ridiculed by all and not least by my father Douglas. School was to be a learning experience on how to perform well. I survived school as a boy relatively easily by attaching myself to two close laddish male friends, Andrew and Denvor, who protected me because I invested heavily in my academic prowess and they respected this aspect of my identity. Yet my Gran also seemed to understand as I mixed the flour for her in a pastry bowl when the boys, as she called her absent sons, were coming home from the Midlands with some money to help out with the family finances. I still feel she seemed to understand that a mistake had been made on 18 May 1949. I feel that I was like one of her daughters: not only did I help her with cooking but I helped her to overcome the increasing disability as the arthritis got worse and she struggled to get dressed. I often went to stay with her, my parents had moved out of Gran's family home to set up a new home for themselves. I have since heard other women talking about their mothers and grandmothers as role models; Gran has been mine, a political and social inspiration, bequeathing to me a keen sense of purpose.

It is not easy to write this, as the memory still feels embarrassing and the risk is still present, despite the success of my struggle against the plethora of horrible experiences resulting from entry 127. My emotions give way to tears as the pain of this struggle re-emerges in my consciousness. Entry 127 can now be amended but history is my reality not the Authority of the Registrar General.

Claire Elizabeth Jenkins: by statutory declaration of the twenty-seventh day of March One thousand nine hundred and ninety six. All the names have been changed, and all the characters are dead now except for me; I have survived.

I try here to make sense of this experience and of the identity I claim as a trans woman. My identity story illustrates how the word 'identity' is used in a commonsense way in several different categories and is my attempt to make some sort of sense of myself now and of my early life. Patricia Gagne *et al* (1997) talk of the value and significance of constructed narratives used to mould current identities. The story is also an attempt to understand why in my life I affiliate with some activities, with whom I affiliate, how I am the same as and different from others and who and what I am – an attempt, as Richard Jenkins has said, 'to know who's who (and what is what)' (2004, p6).

The story opens with the registration of my birth by my mother, an act required by the British nation state where my identities are stamped upon me. There is expressed within the place names *Llwynypia* and *Treorci* an early recognition by me of my Welsh identity, created by cultural acts during my formative years, especially at school and at Cardiff University, where I obtained a physics degree in 1971. My Welsh identity is a collective phenomenon which has largely been created (Morgan, 1981; Williams, 1985; Smith, 1999).

In all these studies, the Welsh are portrayed as a people who have retained some kind of historical identity by constantly and consciously amending their own narrative of nationhood, rather than by the preservation of a dogmatic monoculturalism. In other words, their historical narrative of Welshness can be seen as in a real sense an improvised performance, driven by internal conflict but kept intact by a constantly updated sense of historical tradition (Owen, 2001, p100).

Brubaker and Cooper (2000) would see my Welsh identity as a collective phenomenon, created to instil a sense of solidarity, shared Welsh dispositions and consciousness, especially with regard to and in relation to England, the Other. Kathryn Woodward's (1997) analysis of national identities draws attention to the reinforcing of this national identity through an emphasis on the Other (England in this case) and through symbolism (in the Welsh case, for example, the red dragon). So these early emotional feelings of belonging and of Welsh identity are part of the national performance and symbolism which in more recent years has been foregrounded as being in vogue within Wales.

Indigenous foods like salt marsh lamb are in vogue. And Wales now boasts a national airline, *Awyr Cymru* (pronounced a-wir CUM-ree). *Cymru*, which means 'land of compatriots', is the Welsh name for Wales. The red dragon, the nation's symbol since the time of King Arthur, is everywhere – on T-shirts and bumper stickers, rugby jerseys and even cell phone covers (Worral, 2001, p2).

So I have claim to a contemporary ascendant Welsh identity. The story reveals other aspects of my identity, such as class, bestowed by my father's rank or profession as a general labourer and through childhood residence in the socialist Rhondda, although I have now become more middle-class because I used to be a deputy headteacher before I was forced out of school in order to change sex.

Most important for me has been my paradoxical core identification, my individual psychological and emotional selfhood. This was written upon me in 1949 and is my sexual identity: 'sex is boy.' This stamping of sex upon me was in opposition to the embarrassment of my hidden inner feelings of identification with the opposite collective of female, femininity and womanhood associated here with pretty flowers, aprons, cooking and caring. Sex was cruelly and wrongly assigned to me at birth along with its associated compulsory normative masculine gender.

Authority seizes upon specific material qualities of the flesh, particularly the genitals, as an outward indication of future reproductive potential, constructs this flesh as a sign, and reads it to enculture the body. Gender attribution is compulsory (Stryker, 1994, p249). At birth the usual practice is to inspect the genitalia; presence of a penis indicates boy and labia a female; this identification is subsequently used at registration of birth.

In 1996 I changed my name by statutory declaration and followed this by changing my name on my driving licence and passport. The government informally permits this for transsexual people. The Gender Recognition Act gives transsexual people the legal right to live in their acquired gender. It received its Royal Assent on 1 July 2004 and became law. The act allows transsexual people to amend their birth certificate and therefore legally gives them the rights of other women or men. Included amongst these rights is the right to marry someone of the opposite sex to the acquired gender, so in my case I could marry a man. In 2004 I was still married to a woman and the Gender Recognition Act required that we annul our marriage before I could attain gender recognition and then, if chosen, immediately register a civil partnership as two women. Since 5 December 2005, same sex couples can have their relationships legally recognised. From then on, anyone who registers a civil partnership will have the same rights as a married couple in areas such as tax, social security, inheritance and workplace benefits, but this would have meant that we broke our marriage vows, exchanging a marriage for a partnership. Many married transsexual people find this insulting and refuse to follow this path and remain married and consequently forgo gender recognition. My wife and I took this path but sadly I am now divorced. I now live with a lesbian partner as two women but still my acquired sex remains legally unrecognised in law. Ironically this would allow me to marry my lesbian partner, as legally I am still a man, and forgo a civil partnership.

My partner and a long-term best friend are both Black Caribbean women, second-generation migrants. They are intimate friends with whom I share many of the thoughts, feelings and emotions arising from my gender identification. I feel that we are close because we share a common experience of oppression relating to our embodied identities. They are discriminated against because of their non-normative black skin and me because of my different female body attributes. In addition we share the migratory experience, theirs of crossing cultural boundaries and mine of crossing the gender boundary. We are all renegotiating a new way of life, me amongst women and they amongst White Britons and, as Dave King (2003) points out, we all occupy a position of marginality rather than being fully recognised in our acquired mores.

I have used my identities in different ways. I have a group trans identity; formed as a basis for political action. I have been associated with the social identity movement Press for Change (pfc, 1997-2008), working for about twelve years to further transsexual and transgender rights (transgender is an umbrella term for many types of people whose lifestyles appear to conflict with the gender norms of a society). I am vice chair of the National Union of Teachers' working party on lesbian, gay, bisexual and trans diversity and equality in education, working to pursue these objectives within schools and in the trade union movement. I also identify collectively with Wales; my Welsh dragon is still folded neatly in my chest of draws, ready to break out on March 1, St David's Day, the Welsh national day. I am female; I am an active member of the Church of England Mothers Union. I still identify with my socialist roots as a member of the working class of the 1950s and 60s. The core aspect of my selfhood, my sex, is a basis for my social being and which psychologically and emotionally I feel is abiding and foundational. I also identify as a transsexual woman. Although not explicitly stated in the story, this is implied by transition towards the opposite gender and sex.

I am a transient product of multiple and competing discourses, for example in my life I have been male, female, masculine, feminine, Welsh, English (I have lived in England longer than in Wales), working class, boy, girl and White. Sometimes sorting these out has been painfully confusing, not only for me but also for those around me. I can remember when training to be a counsellor whilst in the early days of my transition, being a man in my family home in the morning, being a woman whilst at university with my fellow trainee counsellors for most of the day, and returning home to have dinner with my family as their father. When I reflexively try to understand my identity I have, I suppose, had a procession of identities: boy, male, teenager, husband, father, heterosexual lover, transgender, transsexual, woman and lesbian; sometimes these are overlapping, sometimes dominating, and always competing. This is my multiple, fluctuating fragmented self of the early 21st century, always fluid and in tension but still retaining a need to hold on to my paradoxical core identification as a woman.

As Kathryn Woodward points out, referring to Stuart Hall:

> Although we may, in common-sense terms, see ourselves as the 'same person' in all our different encounters and interactions, there is also a sense that we are differently positioned at different times and in different places, according to the different social roles we are playing. (Woodward, 1997, p28)

It is impossible to specify a unique nature or essence to the word identity. Its strong use by contemporary social movements in the era of globalisation is important as an alternative to capitalism, consumerism and environmental degradation. Social movements associated with personal identity are also important for personal stability, giving a sense of self in today's rapidly changing world. Craig Calhoun states:

> We know of no people without names, no languages or cultures in which some manner of distinctions between self and other, we and they are not made ... Self-knowledge – always a construction no matter how much it feels like a discovery – is never altogether separable from claims to be known in specific ways by others. (1994, p9-10)

I will continue to use my various identities creatively to survive in this complicated and fragmented world I now inhabit as a woman in order to maximise the quality of my life experiences. I am confident that Gran would be proud of her new granddaughter.

References

Brubaker, R ad Cooper, F (2000) Beyond 'identity.' *Theory and Society* 29(1) p1-47

Calhoun, C (ed) (1994) *Social Theory and the Politics of Identity.* Oxford: Blackwell

Gagné, P, Tewksbury, R and McGaughey, D (1997) Coming out and crossing over: identity formation and proclamation in a transgender community. *Gender and Society* 11(4) p478-508

Jenkins, R (2004) *Social Identity.* London: Routledge

King, D (2003) Gender migration: a sociological analysis (or the leaving of Liverpool). *Sexualities* 6(2) p173-194

Morgan, K O (1981) *Rebirth of a Nation: Wales 1880-1980.* Oxford: Oxford University Press

Owen, R (2001) The play of history: the performance of identity in Welsh historio-graphy and theater. *North American Journal of Welsh Studies* 1(1-2) p101-108

PFC (1997-2008) Press for Change, available at http://www.pfc.org.uk/ (accessed April 2008)

Smith, D (1999) *Wales: A Question for History.* Bridgend: Seren.

Stryker, S (1994) My words to Victor Frankenstein above the village of Chamounix, performing gender rage. *Gay and Lesbian Quarterly* 1(3) p227-254

Williams, G A (1985) *When Was Wales?* London, Black Raven

Woodward, K (1997) *Identity and Difference, (Culture, Media and Identities Series).* London: Sage Publications

Worral, S (2001) *Wales Finding its Voice.* National Geographic 199(June) p62-84

7

Memories of homophobia in childhood: 'social exclusion is not a place where one chooses to hang out'

Mark Vicars

In this chapter Vicars recounts and analyses the experiences of John, a boy whose early attempts to understand and express his emerging sexuality were unsupported by the schools he attended. John's parents recall the ways in which, as Epstein and Johnson put it, schools contributed to pathologising John's gay identity. As John increasingly failed to conform to hetero-gender norms reinforced by his schools, he became increasingly alienated from the school community. Like 'J' from Hinton's chapter, John was diagnosed with behavioural difficulties, raising questions about the extent to which sexuality and gender transgression might contribute to the construction of other school-based pathologies.

Renold's (2005) work on young children's sexualities has challenged the fallacy that children do not have knowledge of sexuality or are not able to articulate anything other than heterosexual identified identities in childhood. However, it can be almost impossible to talk about homosexuality within the context of early childhood education and when such discussions happen they are still deemed controversial, subversive and problematic.

The trouble with being homosexual in educational domains could be that some identities are judged to have more value than others; heterosexuality is invariably perceived as universal and 'natural' whereas other forms of sexuality get thought of as unnatural, odd, perverse and queer. Respondents to Stonewall's (1996) survey of hate crimes indicated that 48 percent of under 18 year-olds had experienced homophobia, 90 percent had been called names because of their perceived sexual orientation and 50 percent of violent attacks had involved fellow students, with 40 percent of those incidents taking place in school.

This chapter draws on parental interviews to tell a story of the impact that homophobia had on their son's education, health and well-being in early childhood and beyond. Throughout his schooling, John (an agreed pseudonym) troubled the presumption of heterosexuality that is so often embedded within the practices and pedagogies of schools. His story suggests that it is almost impossible for queer kids to be seen as anything other than Other when institutional practices are dependent on normalising scripts of identity that work to deposit sexual and any other difference outside of accepted cultural and sexual boundaries.

Through thick and thin

I first met John and his parents when he arrived for an interview on a performing arts course that I was coordinating in a college of further education. At the interview his parents were eager to inform me of John's educational history and they told me that he had been stigmatised throughout his schooling because of his 'sissy boy' behaviour. In the twelve months during which John was a student on the course, I acted as his personal tutor and in tutorials he repeatedly referenced his past experiences of not fitting in. As I listened to his stories, I shared some of my own and throughout our conversations I began to think about how queer identities can find expression within the everyday experiences of educational domains. At the end of the academic year, I approached John to ask if he would be willing to participate in a series of open-ended in-depth interviews in which he would be asked to think about his school experiences in relation to his sexuality. He commented that in the past few months he felt he had moved on and he suggested that I talk to his mum and dad, as they had kept documents relating to his suspensions and exclusions.

I had several lengthy telephone conversations with his parents, who told me about their son's past experiences of homophobia and revealed some of the more disturbing episodes of his self-harm and physical abuse. As rapport between us developed they expressed relief that John was finally getting an education and that since starting the course, he was coming home happy. They remarked that for the first time in a long while he looked forward to going to college and that he was a different person since staring the course. At John's suggestion, I approached his parents at the end of the academic year and asked them if they would be willing to be interviewed about their son's experiences at school. Over a period of two months I conducted six semi-structured interviews in their home.

At our first meeting, John's mother was eager to show the facts of the case and produced a file containing suspensions, exclusions and letters sent from schools that described John's behaviour as being 'of concern'. However, these documents only provided a partial story and as a preliminary interview technique, I asked John's parents to tell me about John's childhood and his and their experiences in relation to his schooling. As they recalled their encounters with educational and child welfare agencies, there were several emotional outbursts ranging from anger directed at John's teachers to anguish at not having been able to have done more to help their son and disbelief at what they had experienced from 'so-called professionals'. As a way of putting experience to work, I followed up each emotional episode with memory priming questions. As Pelias states:

> Memory is volatile. Sometimes, memory's tales just won't do the work they are asked to. They just won't settle, won't arrange themselves so that they might be left alone. They are like scabs itching to be picked. They are wounds always ready to bleed again. (2004, p54)

John's parents recalled the increasing visibility of their son's homosexuality and they referenced how it had created disturbances in the everyday business of the classroom. They spoke about how John preferred to mix and play with the girls and that he presented feminine traits and dispositions from an early age. He refused to play with 'boys' toys' and as his effeminate behaviour became more pronounced the problems that he experienced because he didn't conform to heterogender norms increased. John's parents spoke about how, within their extended family, they sought to cover up and make excuses for his 'sissy boy' behaviour and they talked at length about their fears and anxieties for their son in the past, present and in the future. They spoke of the legacy that verbal abuse and other forms of harassment had on his siblings and described in detail the impact that homophobia had on John's self esteem and explained that they felt it was the cause of his prolonged episodes of self harming and bulimia.

If, as has been suggested, 'identity categories come to be central to how we understand ourselves and others as well as how we understand educational processes and educational inequalities' (Youdell, 2006, p29) then stories of non-normative childhoods may productively reveal the unspoken and disciplining pedagogies of compulsory heterosexuality (Rich, 1993). Bellah *et al* (1986) suggest:

> Stories that make up a tradition contain conceptions of character ... But some stories are not all exemplary, not all about successes and achievements. A genuine community of memory will also tell painful stories ... that sometimes create deeper identities than success. (Bellah *et al*, 1986, p153)

The story that follows was constructed collaboratively and the events described demonstrate how John's behaviour and his parents' attitudes became a troubling presence within hegemonic discourses surrounding childhood and schooling.

Out of the ordinary

I would say that when he went to primary school, that is when it all started. His first teacher would often say to us 'John doesn't mix very well; he would rather play with the girls than with boys'. The school picked up on that immediately, it became an issue of concern for them that he was choosing to mix with girls more than with the boys. We were invited to school and were told that at playtime he would brush and plait the girls' hair. Questions were asked as to why we thought he did this. His teacher asked us about what he did at home and said that we should try and encourage him to play with more boyish toys.

As he got older, he became quite outspoken in class, he started playing up and took to calling his teacher names. Initially, we felt that John's disruptive behaviour was because of his ADHD and we spoke to the doctor about increasing his medication. However, unbeknown to us the name calling at school had got progressively worse and his outbursts were because he felt that his teacher wasn't doing anything about it. John has always been a bit effeminate and he used to come home from school and ask us 'Why are they are all having a go at me?' We tried to be supportive but there was very little at the time that we felt we could do. He was having particular trouble with one lad who kept calling him a pansy. John was getting upset and he would come home from school crying. He had also started messing himself at school because he was afraid of using the toilet but when he started messing himself at home we felt we had to go to the school to sort it. His teacher told us that John wasn't mixing with lads his own age and we explained how he had become wary of the boys in his class because they were calling him names. We told the teacher we thought it was because John might be gay. The next thing we knew we had a social worker at our door.

As his behaviour became more effeminate we were invited in to the school again and told if he didn't calm down and stop being disruptive then we were looking at him being excluded. John ended up attending three primary schools. He was asked to leave the first school when he was in Year 3. It was put to us that he would benefit from a fresh start and in his second school we removed him in Year 6 because of the bullying.

It was around this time, when he was 10, that our phone bill started shooting through the roof. At first we blamed our eldest son, but as the bill was itemised we called a couple of the numbers and they turned out to be gay chat lines. We discussed it with John and he said he had rung them to ask if he was gay and that he had wanted to talk to somebody. What was annoying was that he hadn't come and talked to us. He had taken it upon himself to do something without really understanding the consequences. The thing is, with those chat lines ... that he could have arranged to meet someone and well ... you can imagine the rest. If he had come and talked to us we could have taken him to somebody who knew what he was going through. There was a gay couple who run the local chip shop and we had started talking to them about John. We needed advice and there wasn't anybody in our immediate family we could have talked to about what we thought was happening. We said to John, 'If you feel that you can't really talk to us then you can go to...' but he didn't want to talk to other people, he said it must be something that he was going through, a phase, so we just left it at that. It was at a bonfire night party when he was eleven that he told us how he liked a boy at school, that he found him attractive and that he didn't actually know if he was or wasn't gay.

When he started secondary school it wasn't long before he stopped going completely. He started making himself sick and point blank refused to attend. He told us he didn't want to go to school because of what he had gone through before. The school sent us letters and we went up to see the headteacher to try and sort it out. We gave different reasons; we never said he was gay but eventually we were called in again and this time the deputy head told us about the rumours that had been going around the school. I asked him outright if he had a problem if John was gay. He said 'No, but other pupils do' and that 'If John lashed out then there could be an unpleasant situation'. The school didn't feel that they could put measures in place to prevent that from occurring and it was made to sound as if John was the problem. So we moved him to another school.

However, it wasn't that long before it started all over again and in the end I got sick of it and went to the school and said 'I'm his Dad and I haven't got a problem with it'. We were then called to a meeting about his behaviour and they started by saying they were going to exclude him. They got on about his sexuality, they didn't say he was gay, what they said was, 'Are you aware that he has a problem with his sexuality?' We said, 'He doesn't have a problem and yes we are aware'. This particular teacher was getting on my nerves because he was saying, 'Well, you don't know what your son is getting up to'. And that's what did it; I said, 'You do know that John is gay'. It went quiet and nobody said anything but when they did, they said, 'No, we didn't know but we were aware of something being not quite right but we didn't really know.' I said, 'Well, you do now'.

We had tried all sorts of different ways to deal with what had been going on but we just never had the back-up to fight it or have anybody to help us. At the end of the meeting John was excluded. They kept bringing up his sexuality and in the end I said, 'Excuse me; you are talking about my son, why does his sexuality matter so much to you?' When he went to the next school, the headmaster made it clear that being religious he held certain views and at that point we knew we wouldn't be able to go to that school. However, we did feel reassured because the school had a reputation for being strict; the discipline was good and the headmaster assured us that in his school bullying didn't happen. He said to us that 'While John does have certain feminine ways' we were not to worry about it, '...that would pass when he matured and started to grow up'.

It was about six months later that the problems began again, when John had settled in and started being more open. He had felt that in his new school he was more able to discuss things and started talking about how he was attracted to fellow pupils. The teachers didn't like it and he was taken to the headmaster who told him he didn't want discussions like that in his school and that he should keep his feelings and opinions to himself. There were a lot of incidents at this school, which to be fair were dealt with, but when John was found in a gay chat room on the library computer, we ended up going to see a counsellor at the insistence of the school. We knew John had been contacting gay groups; he used to ring the London gay switchboard and had made contact with two or three regional youth groups. John assured us that he hadn't been looking at pornography and we believed him but eventually we were summoned to school by the headmaster who gave us two options, either John be excluded or leave early in Year 11. His younger brother by this point in time had started to become affected by the situation; he had started getting called names at school because of the attention that his brother was receiving. John left that school early on in Year 11.

Many of the problems John encountered through his school life could have been prevented by the teachers. He stood out from the crowd but the teachers wouldn't take the time to listen to what was going on. They were more ready to protect other kids from John. We have also felt bullied at certain times because of the way some teachers have reacted to us. We needed John to get on academically and when he started on the college course we thought that this time it might be all right.

Reflections

Identities that performatively reiterate normalcy can have a seductive and compelling appeal and the privileges that come with the performance of normalised identities can make them virtually compulsory. Telljohann and Price (1993) have noted how schools often become places where rejection is actively performed and if homophobic bullying is unchallenged then the impact of stigmatisation can lead to higher levels of absenteeism or truancy, resulting in a disrupted education and poor educational achievements. The consequences of embodying sexual differences in educational domains can often be social isolation and victimisation. It would appear from John's experiences that despite the changing attitudes surrounding the discourse on homosexuality in society at large and moves to combat homophobia in education (DfES, 1999; DfES, 2000; DfES, 2004; DCSF, 2007; DfES/DOH, 2004), the coupling of homosexuality and childhood remains problematic. If, as Giroux suggests, 'problematics refer not only to what is included in a worldview, but also to what is left out and silenced' (1988, p4), then in order to overcome the obstacles, difficulties and uncertainties that some teachers may have in addressing sexualities inequalities in schools, a way forward would be to include guidance on sexual diversity on teacher training courses.

Recognising difference in the classroom has to be practised, but this can only be done if educators are able to recognise them. If educators were to recognise that sexuality diversity is as much a social justice issue as gender, class, ethnicity and different abilities are, perhaps some of the barriers to changing heteronormative practices could be overcome. John's story indicates that there is a pressing need to conduct action research that identifies the barriers that prevent sexualities inequalities being addressed by teachers in our schools. His experiences of schooling demonstrate the importance for educators of challenging heteronormative attitudes and practices within school settings. The institutions in John's story didn't know how to overcome the problem except by moving John and 'his problem' on. It is clear from his experience that 'social exclusion is not a place where one chooses to hang out' (Butler, 2002).

Not in my school

A few months ago, I arranged to go into a local primary school to interview the head of personal, health and social education regarding the *Invisible Boundaries: Addressing Sexuality Equality in Children's Worlds* seminar that was to be held at the University of Sheffield. I had hoped to be able to persuade her to speak about the programme she ran in the school and the work the school did on addressing diversity and equality issues. I chose this school because I had been informed by a friend with a child at the school that they were way ahead in developing policies regarding all forms of bullying and discrimination.

The interview began by collecting some background data in terms of number on roll, parental involvement in policy making and so on. Eventually we got round to discussing the issue of inclusion and diversity. Pressing for more information, I was told that in the school there was a one-legged child and, two years before, a child who was a test tube baby. However, when I raised the question of lesbian, gay, bisexual students and their issues, the head of PSHE responded:

> I don't think we have any of those. Besides, we are a Church of England primary school and I don't think it would go down well with the governors and parents if we started talking about that. Anyway, we don't have any in our school and the children are too young to be thinking of such things. I am not sure that the staff would be comfortable dealing with that issue, they don't like doing normal Sex Education at the best of times. We don't do it and it would be very unlikely that we would start to do it.

As I left the interview, I couldn't help but wonder how the school would have responded to John and realised the importance for educators of both finding the courage and having the support in both policy and practice to tackle homophobia in educational domains.

References

Bellah, R, Madsen, R, Sullivan, W and Tipton, S (1986) *Habits of the Hearth: individualism and commitment in American life.* New York: Harper and Row

Butler, J (2002) Is kinship always already heterosexual? *Differences: A Journal of Feminist Cultural Studies* 13(1) p14-44

Department for Children, Schools and Families (2007) *Safe to Learn: Embedding anti-bullying work in schools.* London: Department for Children, Schools and Families

Department for Education and Skills (1999) *Circular 10/99 Social Inclusion: Pupil Support.* London: Department for Education and Employment

Department for Education and Skills (2000) *Sex and Relationships Education Guidance.* London: Department for Education and Employment

Department for Education and Skills (2004) *Every Child Matters: Next Steps.* London: Department for Education and Employment

Department for Education and Skills and Department of Health (2004) *Stand up for Us: Challenging Homophobia in Schools.* London: Department for Education and Skills and Department of Health

Giroux, H (1988) Teachers as Intellectuals: toward a critical pedagogy of learning. NewYork: Bergin and Garvey

Pelias, R (2004) *A Methodology of The Heart: evoking academic and daily life* Walnut Creek: Alta Mira Press

Renold, E (2005) *Girls, Boys and Junior Sexualities: exploring children's gender and sexual relations in the primary school.* London: RoutledgeFalmer

Rich, A (1993) Compulsory heterosexuality and lesbian existence in Compulsory heterosexuality and lesbian existence In Abelove, H, Barale, M and Halperin, M (eds) *The Lesbian and Gay Studies Reader.* London: Routledge

Stonewall (1996) *Queer Bashing: A National Survey of Hate Crimes against Lesbians and Gay Men*

Telljohann, S and Price, J (1993) A qualitative examination of adolescent homosexuals' life experiences: ramifications for secondary school personnel. *Journal of Homosexuality* 26(1) p41-56

Youdell, D (2006) *Impossible Bodies, Impossible Selves: exclusions and student subjectivities.* Dordrecht: Springer

PART THREE

Schools as sites for contesting boundaries

8

A transgender story:
from birth to secondary school

Kate Hinton

Hinton relates the story of J, a child who seemed to understand from a very early age that the gender assigned to him at birth did not adequately describe his identity. This story has been compiled using accounts from several different people, starting with the child's account, moving on to family members and professionals and including the perspective of the author, Hinton, who is Inspector for Equality and Diversity for Children and Young People's Services for a UK local authority. This chapter describes the ways in which J's family and schools worked together to provide an environment where J could thrive rather than suffer the academic exclusion described by Vicars and the experiences of disconnection and secrecy described by Jenkins. Beginning with J's story, we explore in this final section of the book ways in which schools might act as sites for contesting rather than reinforcing boundaries for children in terms of sex-gender-sexuality.

J's story

I was born on 19 July 1996 at York district hospital. I lived in York with my Mam, Dad and brother until I was 18 months old. Then I moved here. A couple of months after I turned 3 my Mam took me to see a doctor because she realised I was lining cars up, playing with certain toys and wearing whatever I wanted to

Author's note: This compilation has retained the original wording of the contributors, which has resulted in some inconsistencies. This is particularly noticeable in the use of the female and male pronoun, which varies according to the source and the phase of education being referred to.

wear (eg trousers and t-shirts). I wouldn't wear what my Mam wanted me to wear (eg skirts, dresses and tights). Whenever she put me in these I just screamed. That's when she took me to see Dr. P.

Dr. P told my Mam I had a form of Aspergers. One year later I started at the local Catholic primary school. While I was in there I wouldn't wear skirts or dresses for my uniform. I wanted to wear boys' trousers and polo shirts, also I didn't want to go swimming because I didn't want to wear swimming costumes or change with the girls. I wanted to wear shorts and change with boys but my headteacher said I couldn't do that so instead of going swimming I stayed at school and did jobs for teachers.

Later in school I had my First Holy Communion coming up and girls needed to wear dresses and boys needed to wear shirts and ties. So instead of wearing a dress or shirts and ties I went and got white trousers, a white t-shirt and white trainers but they were boys' clothing. So my Mam took me back to Dr. P and explained what was going on – then he realised I had Gender Identity Disorder as well as Aspergers.

Now as I am getting older people ask me lots of questions about myself and some people bully me. As I've got older I know how to handle things a bit more because I tell teachers, my parents or sometimes my friends. Sometimes, when I am where no one can find me, I cry or talk to myself.

Mam's story

My daughter was born on 19 July 1996. She was my first-born daughter.

J was a very quiet baby until the age of 18 months. At this age she started showing signs of what I thought was Obsessive Compulsive Disorder. She would line her toys up and only play with cars, people and jigsaws, but what worried me most was the clothes. She would scream at clothes I put on her. She would only wear certain clothes, shoes and hats. I took her to see my health visitor who said it was the start of behavioural problems.

For the next year I struggled along making J wear what I wanted her (him) to wear. I was told not to give in to her at such a young age. So tantrums and tears got part of our life. When J was 2 I left York and moved here. On my second day there we were all (me, dad, J and her brother) invited to a christening. I had bought J a lovely matching dress and hat and bag. I never got to the christening, nor did J. I tumbled with her and tried to hold her down, shouted at her and at one point smacked her hand, but she would not wear the dress. After three hours we both sat crying on the carpet. I gave in but J was happy. I remember her toddling over to me, sitting on my knee and just cuddling me.

Did I learn from that episode? No. J started nursery. I tried again with skirts, tights and bobbles in her hair. Again, we always had tears and tantrums. The bobbles would come out before we got to nursery. I couldn't wait to hand her over. I was drained. Nursery staff loved J, saying she was always really good and never any bother.

When J started at the local Catholic primary school I thought, 'thank God.' She got to wear trousers but hated blouses. The collars were too tight, it was itchy, the list was endless. I would get her to school always late and just hand her over to the headmistress. She became a godsend over the years for me and J. She would give me a cuddle when I was crying and take J. I would walk straight to my health visitor Tracy and cry in her arms.

I got J polo shirts instead of blouses but then the hairstyle began. So off came the lovely blonde bob and in came the short behind the ears. I remember looks and comments I got but I didn't care as J was happy. After two years of horrible, horrible school mornings I was happy too.

J was never called by her female name at school after Year 2. She wouldn't join in 'girly' things and her best mates were all boys she met at nursery and who are still her best mates in secondary school. I remember a school trip J went on to Richmond for a week. When I took her to school that morning she screamed and cried and said she didn't want to go. She went but looking back now, J didn't want to share a dorm with the girls. She wanted to be with the lads.

When J was 4, we were referred as a family to see Dr P at the Child and Family Centre. From what we and J told him, we were told J had a form of autism called Asperger's Syndrome. I remember one session we talked about clothes and I was told to let J wear what she wanted unless we were going out for a special occasion. We tried this and she lived in joggers and t-shirts but when I tried to put her in nice girls' clothes we had the fights and tantrums. I remember J throwing a chair across the room in temper.

When J was 7 I was told by Dr P that it could be the start of Gender Identity Disorder. Finally we knew. So from that day everything I bought for C, J's brother, I bought for J. Out went all the girls' clothes and in came boys' clothes (except underwear).

In Year 6 J's class went swimming. However, she only ever wore shorts and got changed in the boys' changing rooms when we went swimming as a family. So J never went swimming with the school. The headteacher let her stay at school and do 'special jobs'.

Without the headteacher, a transition worker would not have become involved. Also without the headteacher we wouldn't have met KH, the Inspector for Equality and Diversity from the local authority. I think every morning that if we hadn't met these people it would still be tears and tantrums and J not going to school.

Dad's story

I met J when she was 18 months old. She was a cute little girl with wispy hair and always had me in the garden playing football.

The first time I saw J really have a tantrum was when the family moved to this area and we were going to a christening. That day was a battle between J and her mam and I knew who was going to win. You couldn't talk her round, force her or bribe her to wear her dress and hat. She just wasn't going to do it.

This went on for the next few years. I probably didn't see the worst of it because I was out at work before the daily battle began. Her mam took the worst of it – the endless fights getting her ready for school and the meetings with doctors always fell to her. Although I tried, I felt that her mam was probably best to handle it. Maybe that was just an excuse because I really didn't know what to do.

When the gender identity issue was suggested I probably, at first, thought it was a tomboy thing. I had a tomboy in my class in my early years at school who was, to a certain extent, one of the lads. However, there were a few significant differences. The tomboy in my school still wore girls' clothes (with no apparent discomfort), had feminine hair and she left you in no doubt she was a girl. She wasn't a girl who wanted to be a boy, she was a girl who liked playing with the lads, but that was it.

J wants to be a boy. It makes her uncomfortable to be thought of as a girl. It has for many years. It always used to make me smile when a stranger called her 'son' or 'mate'. A smile used to creep across her lips. A sense of satisfaction I think. We soon learned not to correct anyone who made that 'mistake'.

I used to take J to football training with a boy's team. She played for them on a Saturday morning and was very good. The lads in the team had no problem playing with J. They soon knew she gave as good as she got. Unfortunately, she was forced to quit due to FA rules about mixed football teams at age 10. This was the end of her playing football competitively because she could not contemplate playing for an all-girls team. Who makes these rules? J was denied not only playing competitive football but also another leisure activity with her mates was now closed to her.

We had tears and tantrums but not until J was preparing for secondary school did we have the help in changing these daft rules. J was worried, nervous and even afraid, I think, of starting secondary school. Any reassurance we offered probably just seemed like words to J. She was the one who would have to live it. She was the one taking the brave decision of wanting to start school as a boy. The courage to take that step was immense. If she could make a decision like that then the least we could do was to do everything in our power to support her. I was and am afraid for her. I admit I don't fully understand the path she is taking. All I do know is that there are lots of good people who are trying to help her and us as a family to help J have as happy and comfortable school life as possible.

I am under no illusion that the next few years will not be very hard, especially for J. However, I do know that J is determined. She has friends and family that love and support her and want her to feel safe. It is not always easy to live with J but what I do know is that life would be unbearable if she hadn't made this decision. J has taken the first major step on a long road, but having taken that step she has her mam, dad and brother and sisters beside her.

Child Psychiatrist's story

J was referred to the local Child and Adolescent Mental Health Services in December 2000 with 'obsessional' problems, as the family doctor put it. Child Health Services had been involved for some time but there had been no improvement in J's behavioural difficulties and sleep problems.

J and her mother were initially assessed by the senior social worker in the team. J's mother described major tantrums if any rituals at home were broken. However, at school J came across as a well-mannered, pleasant person who enjoyed social contact and had plenty of friends.

I saw J with her mother for the first time in September 2001, when J would have been just over 5 years old. J's mother was worried about her obsessions and rituals. The major obsession was J's wish to act and behave like a boy and her Mum was worried that J thought she was a boy. For at least 18 months J had wanted boys' toys and wanted to wear boys' clothes. J would line up toys and liked a set routine and to be in control. This seemed to be beyond that of a normal child and Mum wondered if it was hormonal. She was also worried that she might be being too strict a disciplinarian with J. I explained to mum that there may be features of an Autism Spectrum Disorder, probably Asperger's Disorder. Considering J's young age, it was difficult to diagnose transvestism or a transsexual condition (my words at that time!), and it was agreed that I should follow her up at regular but infrequent intervals.

In 2003 J, a consultant paediatrician, J's mother and I met. By now, J's mother had accepted J's wishes to wear boys' clothes and she commented that J even walks like a boy. We wondered if J's behaviour was part of Asperger's Disorder or something separate. J's mum requested blood tests for hormone levels and the results were in the normal range. J was followed up regularly in 2003/04 when the diagnosis of Gender Identity Disorder was raised. By mid-2004 J's mother had accepted J's ways and J was much happier in herself and socially more comfortable, although she continued to be bounded by routine and had become a perfectionist in many aspects of her life. The small primary school J attended was very accommodating of her, but J's mother was worried about the future move to secondary school.

During the regular sessions in early 2007 we discussed how best to get help for J's Gender Identity Disorder and whether to disclose the gender issues at this stage or leave it until later. Throughout this period, apart from one session when doubts were expressed, J was clear in her identity as a boy, so it was agreed that she would start secondary school as a boy. A number of aspects of the move to secondary school, such as gender identity, uniform, toilets, PE [Physical Education] and swimming, were causing J considerable anxiety. Before the end of the summer term, detailed plans for the transition were drawn up through meetings of the parents and professionals from education and health.

Around the same time, a referral was organised to the Gender Identity Development Service at the Portman Clinic, London. The Primary Care Trust readily made available the funding for the referral.

J is accepted as a boy in the secondary school and has settled in well. What remains to be addressed over the next few years is how best to help J manage the emotional aspects of adapting to a different gender. It is hoped that J's temperamental resilience and sociability will help the process of major change ahead for him. The support of J's family, his mother in particular, continues to be a real strength and there is a high level of professional commitment towards helping J. I wish him well for the future.

Primary headteacher's story

My first memory of J was as a child in the infants. She was very polite, friendly and popular with staff and pupils but even from a very early age demonstrated some behaviours of a confused child.

Occasionally she would be late for school and her mother would ring to explain that J had simply refused to wear a particular item of clothing or shoes. I could hear her screaming and shouting in the background (not at all like the lovely child

I knew in school!). When J came into school she would merely look down when she went past me but then proceeded to join in with the other children as if nothing had even happened. Basically, an understanding developed that J could sometimes act like this but generally not in school. Such tantrums stopped around the age of 6.

We did however make a major mistake in casting J as Mary in the Key Stage 1 [5-7 year-olds] Nativity. We took into consideration that J was a 'tomboy' and most of her friends were boys and that we knew she would not want a frivolous outfit such as a snowflake or angel. We had not anticipated J's outright refusal to wear anything resembling a dress! I can remember staff persuading J that it was a gown just like those of the shepherds or Joseph but was just plain blue. She played the part well – but reluctantly!

Throughout J's primary school years our understanding of her grew and developed. She was mature for her age and became able to convey her worries more easily.

As the age of 7, J was ready to start preparations for First Holy Communion. At the very beginning of the year she said that she wanted to take part but would not under any circumstances wear a dress. I told her it did not matter what she wore and she could wear trousers if she wanted. In the event she was an asset to the group, wearing a white trouser suit and a broad smile. I was very proud of her that day!

Towards the end of her primary school years issues arose and were dealt with. In retrospect some might have been handled better, but perhaps not.

Over the years J's Mum kept me informed on issues raised with the consultant paediatrician but we didn't receive any written reports at this stage as it was generally believed that J would start facing decisions at puberty and as a young adult.

The school nurse was aware that J was special, liaising with her before giving Puberty Talks to her class, since we believed that this could potentially unsettle J.

J was very much 'one of the boys' by this time. Her friends were boys and she was an excellent football player. Her voice started to deepen slightly and facially she looked like a very good looking boy! Everyone in school just knew her as J and loved her for who she was.

At the beginning of Year 6 it became evident that J was going to have to make decisions earlier rather than later. She was very aware that she was different and was extremely worried at the prospect of moving on to secondary school. We alerted the secondary school through the Transition Coordinator, who established excellent links with J and her family.

J had a very emotional year but was mature enough to access the support available. She was able to express her fears and share them with others. She became quite sure about what she wanted and what she didn't, but was extremely worried at the potential hurdles she might face.

J became determined to be treated as a boy at secondary school. I was desperately worried that at the beginning of the summer term major decisions and subsequent preparations still needed to be made. However, by the end of the summer term real progress had been made. I had my reassurances that J was going to be protected and supported in her new school.

I am kept informed about how J is doing. I must admit that I find it difficult when the secondary school staff refer to J as 'he' and I tend to say 'she' – but I will get used to it. All I know for certain is that J is a very special person!

Inspector's story [Inspector for Equality and Diversity and chapter author]

I was alerted to J's transition to secondary school by the primary headteacher and my PE colleague. By then some messages had arrived in the secondary school about J and her very strong desire to do PE with the boys. The PE department was very concerned about this, both on health and safety grounds and because the sports councils, especially the Football Association, advised that after the age of 11 boys and girls should not play mixed sport. I met J and also attended multi-agency casework meetings at which J's requests were clarified.

At this stage the biggest stumbling block was the arrangements for PE and I felt it was imperative that these were resolved before the end of the summer term. I contacted a range of national bodies in the sporting field, the Equal Opportunities Commission, the DfES [Department for Education and Skills] and transgender agencies. None of them were able to give a clear lead, largely because they had not come across such a young transgender child. The youngest age I managed to find official information about was 16. I did have some very helpful conversations with transgender agencies, such as Mermaids, and was well supported locally.

After taking advice from the County Council Health and Safety and Legal teams, my PE colleague and I came to the conclusion that there were no strong grounds for not meeting J's request and that, under current legislation, it could constitute discrimination not to do so. We therefore strongly advised the school and PE department to include J in boys' sport and this was agreed for Year 7 in the first instance, just before the beginning of the summer holiday.

Also before the end of the summer term, J made additional visits to the secondary school, met her form tutor and made plans for other matters such as her uniform, appropriate changing and toilet facilities and how the form tutor would provide daily support. An important issue we debated was which staff should be briefed and how. It was agreed that all the staff needed briefing so Dr. P and I prepared a paper for the school to use as a basis at the start of the autumn term. At the start of each year, when staff are briefed about pupils with Special Educational Needs, they are told that J is to be treated as a boy and that further details are available from the form tutor.

The review at the end of the first term showed that J and his mum were very pleased with the way the school had responded to J's needs and especially the way the form tutor had supported him. J had missed some school time, partly for a family holiday, but teachers felt that he was making good progress across the curriculum. The PE department had no concerns about J doing all his sport with boys, although he cannot play in football teams outside the school. Partly as a result of this and difficulties over swimming, there was concern about J's social life outside the school. The family and professionals agreed to look into other more suitable physical activities.

By the end of the first year J was much happier, with new friends, a social life outside school and good progress with school work. Staff were entirely comfortable with all the arrangements and keen to continue these for the next year. Importantly, the form tutor will be the same and will continue to provide the essential support for J and regular communication with Mum.

J's story

Moving on to secondary school, things changed because it isn't mixed PE any more and female and male uniforms aren't the same. So me and my Mam fought for me to go into secondary school as a boy and for me to do male PE. Also, she even fought for me to have my own toilet.

Me and my Mam won the battles so I can do male PE and sports. I am treated as a boy in the school and I can wear the boys' uniform. But another person who has been amazing and helped me is my form tutor. She has helped me because she has given me passes to come out of class when I feel down in the dumps and she found me my own toilet and the keys for it. Also she lets me use the teachers' toilet in the reception area to get changed for PE and sports.

Form tutor's story

The school became aware of J's situation through our transition worker who works with the Year 6 pupils in our feeder primary schools. We then liaised with the Educational Psychology Service who advised us to consult the medical professionals dealing with J's case. We questioned whether J should have a SEN [Social and Emotional Needs] statement and were told that this was not necessary. In light of this advice, the school organised the first of a series of meetings which involved J's parents, representatives from a number of outside agencies and school staff. The main issue was J entering school as a boy and the implications for uniform, toilet and changing facilities and PE (which is taught as a single sex subject in Key Stage 3, ages 11-14). Another consideration was that in primary school J had been known as a girl and so would be known to some pupils as a girl.

Throughout this process the school sought guidance from relevant government and sporting bodies, which took a good deal of time, as many had no experience of working with pupils in J's situation. We used the information and advice we could procure to develop a transition plan which outlined that J would enter as a boy and wear the boys' uniform. He would be given access to a disabled toilet and changing facility and would participate fully in PE as a boy. It was decided to brief the whole staff on J's situation. They were advised that J would be joining the school as a boy and was to be treated accordingly. It was necessary to ensure that all registers and set lists had the correct name and did not refer to gender.

J joined the school in September and his transition has gone extremely well. He was given a time-out card which included my timetable so he could leave lessons discreetly if he needed to and could also gain access to his form room at break times. I also pointed out other safe points around the school, such as the SEN department. Pupils who knew J at primary school asked a few questions but these were born of curiosity rather than malice. These pupils were immediately referred to me so I could speak to them promptly and forestall potential difficulties. I was in daily contact with J's mum so I could obtain a progress report and deal with any issues immediately. One problem we encountered was that the disabled toilet that J was using was in quite a prominent position so he was worried about going in and out when other pupils were around. We considered other facilities and found more satisfactory alternatives for both toilet and changing facilities.

Staff still need to be proactive in their outlook to ensure that problems do not arise, for example by making sure that exam papers don't state 'female' or that outside agencies (eg. eye tests, photographs) don't call out his full name. However, mistakes have been minimal and this has allowed J to integrate fully into his new school and form class. He has established a new friendship group and is a popular member of his form. Although we still take it day by day J is rapidly growing in confidence and is embracing life in secondary school. Arrangements for sport and PE are working well and the PE staff have no concerns at present.

Mum's story: September 2007 – March 2008

J started secondary school as a boy and this was fine, but we were told that she/he (I should say J is now referred to as he/male and I'm 100 percent happy with this, but get a kick up the butt because I keep saying she/her), wouldn't be allowed to do boys' sports, only girls' sports. This was devastating to J. J was allowed to wear a tie (the boys wear ties but not the girls). Thanks to KH looking into the sports issue for us we were finally told that J could do boys' sports.

J never uses female toilets so has been given her own toilet and changing room. She has a pass that allows her to leave her class any time without being questioned. Before J started secondary school we had six weeks of no sleep, tears, bed-wetting and nightmares. J was worried about bullying, toilets, PE, etc...

J's first day at secondary school went really well and the first term went better than any of us could have imagined. J has gone in as a boy and now has two toilets he can use. There have been incidents of name calling and J getting wound up and upset but I speak to his form teacher every day after school so she is aware of what has happened before she gets into school the next day. J gets more confident every day about going to school as a boy. This is the best thing that could happen at this time in his life.

I would like to add that J's form teacher has become a friend as well as a fine teacher to us. With her help the transition has gone really well. I have her home and mobile phone numbers and she has told us we can contact her 24/7. I don't think many teachers would show this level of commitment. I have struggled for eleven years so this cannot be easy for the form tutor, but she has done whatever she can for us. We have complete trust in her.

After a difficult patch in January, J is finding strength daily and we, his family, feel proud of him. But most importantly J feels proud of himself, is taking full part in school life and is making new friends.

We as a family are now travelling to London to the Portman Clinic, where we see Gender Specialists. J's future is in their hands for the next few years and there are big questions about puberty and the use of hormone blocks. We all know puberty will not be easy and nor will telling new friends. But whatever happens, we as a family will love and support J until he attains his dream of becoming a young man.

Appendix:
Working with a Transgender Pupil

These notes were compiled for the secondary school in readiness for J's arrival in September 2007. They were prepared by Kate Hinton in consultation with Dr Prasad, the Child Psychiatrist working with J. Since then, some changes of wording have been made following further consultation with Jay Stewart of Gendered Intelligence.

Guidance for school staff

This is an unusual case, largely on account of the pupil's young age, and there are almost no examples nationally to draw from. It is really important that the school, the Local Authority and the medical profession do all we can to support the pupil through adolescence and to make good educational progress.

Some useful terms

Sex is assigned at birth and is based on the appearance of genitalia. The body has sexed chromosomes and hormones which control the development of external genitalia, internal sex organs and secondary sexual characteristics. They may also influence the way areas of the brain develop in males and females.

Gender identity refers to the roles and attributes associated with sex and the related social shaping of an individual as being a girl or a boy. It is used to describe the inner feeling of being a girl/woman or boy/man.

Gender role describes how we are expected to behave in society as boys or girls, men or women.

Female to male refers to a person who is assigned female at birth but is male in terms of gender identity. This applies to the pupil who is joining the school.

What is the transgender/transsexual condition?

Very occasionally babies are born with a mismatch between their physical and psychological genders. This may be because the development of the brain has progressed along a different pathway from the rest of the embryo's body and can be felt in early childhood. The result is great discomfort for the individual with their gender identity and most transgender people struggle with questions about how best to live their lives. For some adults this will lead to gender reassignment, so they can be seen socially as their preferred gender.

This is entirely separate from sexual orientation (lesbian, gay, bisexual inclinations) and from transvestism (enjoying dressing in the clothes of the opposite sex).

Living as a transgender/transsexual person

Given the importance of sex and gender in our sense of identity, especially as adolescents, being transgender is not easy for the individual to live with. There is almost bound to be confusion and upset, which is nobody's fault. What is important is that adults and peers do all they can to support the individual through this uncertain time. The parents in this case are very supportive of the child. Additionally, we now have anti-discriminatory legislation for transgender and transsexual people, several specialist support agencies and changing social attitudes. However, there is no blueprint so we all need to explore and gradually learn the best ways to behave.

Some starting points for all staff

- The school has already agreed to the pupil's request to dress in the boys' uniform, to do PE and sport with boys during Year 7, to be treated as a boy in other contexts and to use the disabled toilet

- Keep gender-related practices to a minimum (eg girls' and boys' groups)

- Avoid gender-stereotyped comments (eg boys don't cry, that isn't very lady-like)

- Draw minimumal attention to the pupil being in any way different

- Avoid judgemental opinions about the pupil's identity conflicts, appearance or behaviour

- Look out for teasing, gossiping or bullying and take all instances seriously

- Ensure that the pupil is not left out of activities in lessons and during break and lunch

- Use the form tutor as the main source of support for the pupil

- Offer time out if the pupil is distressed

- Be tolerant of uncertainty, confusion and distress – they are bound to occur

- Be positive about the pupil's achievements and personal qualities

- Focus on short-term goals which are achievable

- Help to sustain self esteem and hope

- Be consistent and introduce as little change as possible to routines

- If other pupils ask questions, briefly say: *The pupil feels he is a boy and wants to be treated as one*

9

Commentary on J's story

Jay Stewart

Stewart's chapter provides specific commentary on Hinton's story of J as well as some broader understandings about trans identities and the ways in which they might be supported by schools ad other institutions. Stewart is co-founder of the organisation Gendered Intelligence (www. genderedintelligence.co.uk). He urges us to remember that not all trans experiences are the same, and that gender variant, or gender queer, people include a diverse range of people whose gender identity and/or presentation does not conform to social norms that categorically define sex/gender in particular ways. Further critical analysis of these socially constructed sex/gender categories and the ways in which sexuality tends to be conflated with them, is provided by DePalma and Atkinson in their chapter on heteronormativity.

J's story is a compelling and moving account of a young trans boy's journey through his primary school years. It is particularly striking because of the different viewpoints that are incorporated, all of which offer an overall picture of a person's growing identity. In some ways this is a run-of-the-mill growing up story – the battle of wills between child and parent, the contradictory versions of who someone is, or how that person's behaviour varies according to the surrounding environment or people. However, J's coming into his own identity, and his expressions of that identity, force us to question our social expectations of gendered behaviour.

Like many stories about trans and gender variant people[1], this story draws attention to the ways in which we divide the world into boys and girls, men and women, often in a mundane way. Trans is sometimes thought to be complicated because a trans person does not fit easily into these categories. Indeed trans identities ask us to question the very terms 'girl' and 'boy'. For example, J's rebellion against having to wear 'matching dress and hat and bag' usually makes people ask *what is wrong with the person who refuses to dress this way?* But maybe we should ask *why should J be expected to wear these things at all?*

Everyone has a unique past, experience and journey when coming out and living as trans. My own story, for example, has been very different from J's. Although I felt very angry about the various social expectations of being a girl and how I should therefore dress and behave, I did not express these feelings as: 'I am a boy'. For myself it was not until I was in my late 20s that I came out as trans, but before that I had identified as a lesbian. Importantly for me, having identified as a lesbian is something that I am just as proud of as being a trans man now. Because there are so few stories of trans people, in particular under the age of 11, it is vital that we do not take one story and apply it across the board to all trans people.

What is most striking in J's story is the exceptional working together across the agencies and services of education and health care. There is a lot of good practice here that others can learn from. The approach has been pragmatic and based around problem-solving, for example finding suitable toilets for J. It is important to reflect on the various constraints within the gender binary and to ask if they are necessary – and not only for those who identify as trans or gender variant. Rethinking the norms around clothing, toilet use, playground activities and so on can make schools more inclusive places for *all* children.

Education is also absolutely key if we are to improve the experience of young trans people in and outside schools. People are afraid of what they don't know and it is the fear which is most damaging. It is evident in the story of J that those close to the trans person also need information and support, particularly family members, whose thoughts, emotions and questions also need recognising. Here we also see how the teachers and headteacher have gained in knowledge and confidence through this experience, but such education should not be limited to those lucky enough to come across characters as strong as J. Other young trans people are not so self-assured and their teachers may not have the opportunities to learn about gender diversity.

There is a lot to be learnt from J's story, but I am left wondering what the future holds for him. J has fought so hard to achieve so much already! His story demonstrates how being treated and seen as the person and the gender in which you see yourself as is absolutely crucial. I hope, however, that this does not mean that J feels he has to hide his trans status. Secondary school can be a place where being different in any way is often very hard. I wonder if J feels he can be out as trans? I hope for J and others like him, including myself, that we can work towards a world where we can be treated and seen as both transmen and simply as men, and that knowing of our trans identities does not compromise how others interact with us on a day-to-day basis.

I have been part of the trans community since 2002. In 2006 I co-founded Gendered Intelligence, an organisation that brings young trans people together. The Internet is a great resource for young trans people to find out information and chat on line. However our approach at Gendered Intelligence is based on the belief that it is important to come together and meet other trans people to talk in the flesh about our experiences. So far we have worked with nearly 40 young trans people between the ages of 14 and 22 from across the UK. Young trans people need to know that they are not alone and that there is nothing wrong with being trans.

Information, support and knowledge around trans and gender variance is growing. More and more trans people are coming out as trans and doing so at a younger and younger age. It is important that trans and gender variant people, just like LGB young people, are supported in school. How we do that is something that we are only just starting to think about. For example, focusing on anti-homophobic bullying measures in many ways leaves out trans and gender variant people and some of their needs can go unacknowledged. Because of this Gendered Intelligence also works in schools, colleges and non-statutory settings with non-trans young people, in order to develop an understanding that gender identities and expressions are diverse, rich and multiple.

Note

1 Trans is an umbrella term. It includes cross-dressers, transgender and transsexual people and anyone else who is in any way gender variant. A transsexual person usually chooses to use medical intervention in order to align their body with their mind, their outside appearance with their internal feelings. A transgendered person might wish not to have medical intervention. A cross-dresser is someone who likes to wear clothes usually associated with the 'opposite' gender. Other gender variant people can identify as both sexes or outside of or other to the identities of male or female, or they may present themselves in a way that goes against the social norms for their biological sexed identity. Gender variant can also be known as Gender Queer.

10

Building allies against exclusion and oppression: teaching young children to take a stand

Mara Sapon-Shevin

Sapon-Shevin reminds us that exclusion, whether on the basis of gender, sexuality, race, disability or some other perceived difference, is an aspect of school culture that can be changed, and should be changed, for the benefit of all pupils. Echoing Sander's assertion that racist and homophobic bullying is caused by racism and homophobia (rather than a particular race or sexuality), Sapon-Shevin argues that exclusion is not about difference; it is about our responses to difference. She offers some concrete examples of activities, songs, and books that can be used in the primary classroom to help foster socially just communities in which all people are valued and safe. Together with Hinton and Watkins, Sapon-Shevin demonstrates that when teachers and senior management take seriously their responsibilities to examining their curriculum, their pedagogy and the classroom climate, they can make changes in children's worlds.

There is little argument that we live in violent and challenging times. The media abounds with stories of bullying, harassment, hate crimes and school violence. Addressing these issues with young children may seem overwhelming. We might ask, 'Aren't they too young to understand and respond to such complex societal issues?'

This chapter presents an answer to this question as follows: It is never too early to raise issues of social justice with children, and it is possible to do so in ways that are both age-appropriate and engaging. Learning the vocabulary of social justice and beginning to see oneself as an ally in the face of oppressive behaviour are both possible and desirable goals for children as young as pre-school aged (Sapon-Shevin, 2007).

Here I share ways of using children's literature, music and movement to explore these issues with children and to empower their teachers and care-givers to commit to this important work (Sapon-Shevin, 1999).

Exclusion

'You can't be in our group!' 'Let's not let Lilly be on our team/in our club/at our party.' 'You're not my friend – I don't play with people like you.' Although we associate those phrases with childhood experiences, many adults have also experienced – and may still experience – exclusion on the basis of race, age, sex, family background, class, sexual orientation, religion, language or physical characteristics.

Who among us hasn't been left out at some point? The party to which we weren't invited, the people sitting together at lunch who made it clear we weren't welcome at the table and the more subtle exclusions of disregard and invisibility are all painfully familiar to many of us. Exclusion, however, is not about race or language or gender – or any other difference. Rather, the culture of exclusion posits that isolating and marginalising the stranger or the the outlier is appropriate, acceptable, and sometimes even laudatory. Exclusion is not about difference; it is about our responses to difference. How can this be explored with young children? I propose several strategies.

Cycles of exclusion
- Ask pupils to write down a time they were excluded and a time they excluded someone else.
- Then have them write what their feelings were in each of these situations.
- Make a list on the board or on chart paper of 'Feelings when I was excluded' and 'Feelings when I excluded others.'
- Discuss the two lists, and how they are the same and different.

It has been my experience that nearly everyone can recall instances in which they were excluded or excluded others. There is no us and them; it is just us. Although the feelings in both lists are not necessarily the same, they are usually negative. Pupils report that when they were excluded they felt hurt, scared, embarrassed, angry, rejected, sad and worthless. They also report, however, that even when they were the ones doing the excluding, they usually didn't feel that great; some report that at first they felt powerful or triumphant, but later guilty, ashamed, or bad about themselves. Use the discussion as an opportunity to talk about how exclusion feels and why pupils exclude others.

Exclusion snapshots
- Have pupils share, in groups of three or four, their exclusion stories.

- Have each group choose one of the stories to represent visually.

- Have them construct a snapshot of what the exclusion looked like. It might be two children talking with their backs to a third, or perhaps two children whispering about another.

- Then have them imagine what an inclusion snapshot would look like and how they could represent it.

- Have each group share their snapshots with the rest of the class, moving from their exclusion snapshot to their inclusion snapshot.

- Have pupils discuss what they noticed about each and how the snapshot made them feel.

It can be very powerful for pupils to use their bodies in creating and re-creating exclusion and inclusion. The discussion afterwards is likely to be much richer than it would be if the experience were only analysed verbally.

Children's book: *This is Our House* by Michael Rosen and Bob Graham, 2005
In this children's book, George has a house made from a big cardboard box and he says that no one else at the playground can come in. He systematically excludes children on the basis of gender, size, and other

characteristics, telling each in turn, 'This house isn't for girls, for people who wear glasses, for twins', and so on. But when George leaves his house for a moment, everyone piles in, and on his return, George understands what it means to be excluded and decides that the house is for everyone.

- ■ Read the book to the class and discuss what they think should happen after each incidence of exclusion.

- ■ Have the children act out the book, assigning the various roles in it to children, without regard to their own characteristics.

- ■ Brainstorm, as a class, all the ways in which various aspects of classroom life could be shared. Encourage creative problem-solving if children insist, 'But only one person can fit on the swing', or 'There isn't room for everyone.'

Many teachers hesitate to initiate such discussions because they fear making issues of exclusion worse. They hope that by not talking about the way children are treating a particular child badly, somehow the problem will go away. Or they fear that they lack the skills or the classroom norms for such a discussion. These concerns are genuine and worthy of our attention, but if we wait until everyone feels ready to address them, we may wait a very long time. Failing to address what all the pupils have already observed communicates that exclusion is inevitable. Even imperfect attempts at challenging exclusion can communicate that the way in which we treat one another matters and that doing so in the classroom is a priority worthy of our time and attention.

Teasing

Teasing is a pervasive problem in most school environments. Although the form the teasing takes may differ, including new possibilities occasioned by the internet and cyber-bullying, name-calling and harassment are unfortunately quite common. There are, however, ways of addressing this issue with children of all ages.

Teachers of young children rarely need convincing that the social climate of the classroom is crucial to pupils' development and learning. Teachers of older pupils often feel constrained by curricula that choke out time for attending to the classroom's social climate. At a time when high-stakes testing and narrowly-constrained notions of 'standards' are impairing teachers' ability to focus on what matters most to their pupils, we need to support teachers' attention to teasing and bullying. Creating pupils who can pass tests but who treat one another cruelly or indifferently is not a formula for successful schooling nor for a democratic society.

How does it feel? What shall we do?

■ Ask pupils to describe times when they were teased and how it felt.

■ Make a list of all the things the children have been teased about: weight, skin colour, size, gender, physical abilities, school performance, language, religion, and so on

■ As a class, establish classroom rules regarding:

a. how teasing will be addressed in the classroom.

b. what pupils should do if they have been teased.

c. what pupils can do if they see someone else being teased.

Children's book: *Chrysanthemum* by Kevin Henkes, 1991

In the children's book *Chrysanthemum* pupils tease Chrysanthemum about her name. The first teacher, Mrs. Chud, tells the children to put their heads down and she attempts to ignore the behaviour, which, not surprisingly, escalates. The second teacher, Mrs. Twinkle, not only notices the pupils' teasing, but inquires about it and responds to the teasers in a thoughtful, productive and non-punitive way.

■ Read the book to children and discuss the story.

■ Ask the children to share their names, including what their name means, after whom they were named, what they want to be called, and so on.

■ Ask the pupils to discuss what they could do if they witnessed another child being teased about their name or other personal characteristics.

Was that funny? looking at humour

One of the most age-appropriate ways to discuss issues of oppression with pupils relates to jokes. Encourage them to listen carefully to the jokes they hear being told and those they tell, for examples of racism, sexism, homophobia, disability oppression and the like. The groups that are singled out for derision are often culturally and historically specific. Whole generations of jokes (moron jokes, Polish jokes in the US, Irish jokes in the UK, blonde jokes, etc.) are testimony to the pervasiveness of oppression passed off as humour. What can you say or do if the joke-teller is your parent, your teacher, a popular student in the class, your boss? Are there funny jokes that don't make fun of people? What are some possible responses to oppressive humour?

Talk to pupils about ways to interrupt oppressive jokes in ways that work for them. Challenge pupils to bring in jokes to share that aren't oppressive. Have a weekly joke time to reinforce the idea that it is possible to have fun and be funny without hurting people or reinforcing discrimination and oppression.

Becoming allies

It is important for pupils to understand that both historically and currently, not all people are treated fairly in society. Based on the age and maturity of the pupils, the language and examples used will vary, but teachers should be able to find ways of explaining different forms of injustice so that children can relate and understand. Having pupils bring in news articles or jokes that evidence oppression or discrimination can be a fine starting point and so can children's own observations of their school, neighbourhood and community.

After leading pupils in a discussion about the ways children and adults are discriminated against, the next question is, 'So what do I do if I notice this happening?'

What do I do?

One useful way to begin the discussion with young children is as follows:

- ◼ Seat pupils in a circle and go over some of the 'isms', such as sexism, racism, homophobia. This might follow an incident that has occurred in the classroom or the community.

100

- Ask pupils to think of times when they witnessed some kind of oppression. This might be someone ignoring a child who is waiting to be served in favour of an adult (adultism), making a racial slur about African-Americans (racism), one student calling another a 'faggot' or a 'lezzie' (homophobia) and so on.

- Then ask pupils to think about a time when they took action or did not take action, and ask them share their story with a partner. Ask pupils to consider the following, 'Why did you feel comfortable or uncomfortable speaking up?' Pupils might share issues of power ('It was my teacher who said something sexist, so I didn't know what to say'), relationships ('It was someone I'm good friends with, and I knew it would be okay even if he got mad at me right then for telling him not to do that') or knowledge ('I knew it was wrong, but I didn't know what to do or say', or 'I was afraid that if I said something I'd get in trouble or make it worse').

- From there, engage the pupils in role-plays or discussion about how they can interrupt bullying or other oppressive behaviours, using their own experiences or provided examples:

    a. You're on the playground and one of your friends tells you not to invite Marcus to be in the game because he's a 'homo.' What do you do?

    b. Three of you are planning what to do over the weekend, and one of your friends proposes a plan that you know the third person won't be able to afford. What do you say?

    c. One of the pupils in your reading group starts making fun of a student in a lower reading group, calling him a 'retard' and telling him he reads 'baby books.'

    d. With the pupils, generate a list of things they might say when they see an injustice being perpetrated.

Children's book: *Hey Little Ant* by Phil Hoose and Hanna Hoose, 1998
This picture book, based on a song with the same title, has been translated into eight languages. It is a dialogue between a child and an ant, which begins with the child threatening to squash the ant flat. The

ant asks, 'If you were me and I were you, what you would want me to do?' The illustration shows an enormous ant and a tiny little boy.

After hearing or reading the song, have small groups discuss the following:

- How would you feel if you were the ant?
- How would you feel if you were the child?
- What should the child do?

Small groups of pupils can act out the song using the ending they have decided on. Pupils could also role-play what they might say to the would-be ant-squishing boy, or they could practice their writing skills by writing a letter to the boy telling him what they think he should do or not do to the ant and why.

The story sparks class discussions of ways in which pupils have treated others and been treated by others on the basis of differences in size, identity, or other characteristics. With older pupils, such discussions can centre on ways in which groups within the community treat one another, including those in different neighbourhoods, gangs, or racial and ethnic groups (see www.heylittleant.com).

Children's book: *Say Something* by Peggy Moss, 2004
In this book, a young girl witnesses the mistreatment of her classmates: pupils who are teased, pushed in the hallways and excluded at lunch and on the bus. Although she is troubled by the way the children are treated, she is somewhat self-congratulatory about her own stance, saying, 'I don't do that', 'I don't say that.' Then at lunch one day the girl has to sit alone and she becomes the object of painful teasing herself. She struggles not to cry, and then, when she does cry, the other kids tease her even more. She wishes she could disappear.

After her tormentors leave, she sees that there are kids she knows sitting nearby who have witnessed her mistreatment. She sees on their faces that they feel sorry for her, but she is stunned that they said nothing while she was being bullied. When she goes home and tells her brother she is angry at the kids at the other table, he says, 'Why? They didn't do anything.' 'Right', she says. In that moment, it becomes clear to her – and the reader – that silence is collusion; that not saying anything is a very loud response. The next day, she sits next to the girl on the bus who has been excluded.

The book is a powerful starting point for a discussion about taking a stand and saying something or doing something rather than being a passive observer. Discuss the book with pupils and have them practice what they might say or do when they witness mistreatment in their school or classroom.

Children's song: 'Courage' (Bob Blue)
Bob Blue's song 'Courage' tells the story of a girl who witnesses the exclusion of a classmate, Diane. She makes connections between Diane's exclusion and a recent social studies lessons about 'gas chambers, bombers, and guns in Auschwitz, Japan, and My Lai' and about the fact that many stood by silently. At the end of the song she says:

> I promise to do what I can
> to not let it happen again.
> To care for all women and men,
> I'll start by inviting Diane.

Pupils respond strongly to this song, and are more than eager to discuss their own experiences of exclusion and their responses. Pupils can and do respond with courage to exclusion and bullying. Play the song for pupils (or share the words) and ask:

- How did this song make you feel?

- What memories did it bring up for you?

- Has there ever been a time when you felt like you didn't have friends or were being treated unfairly?

- What kinds of support would you want from people if you were in that situation?

- Have you ever seen someone being treated unfairly? What did you do? If you didn't do anything, what kept you from doing something?

I will stand up, I will ask why
There is a famous quote from Pastor Martin Niemöller, written after the Holocaust:

First they came for the Communists,
and I did not speak out because I was not a Communist.

Then they came for the trade unionists,
and I did not speak out because I was not a trade unionist.
Then they came for the Jews,
and I did not speak out because I was not a Jew.
Then they came for me,
and there was no one left to speak out for me. (Niemöller, 1946)

Discuss this quote with pupils:

- What do you think it was like during the Holocaust for members of the targeted groups?

- What do you think it was like for members of the dominant group?

- Where and how did people in Nazi Germany learn about Jews, people with disabilities, homosexuals? How do you think this affected their willingness and ability to be allies to those who were being targeted and killed?

Then share this contrastive song, 'Stand up' written by Mike Stern with additional lyrics by Charlie Kind and Karen Brandow:

First they came for the Communities,
They they came for the Jews
But I wasn't a Communist
And I wasn't a Jew
So I didn't stand up
And I didn't ask why
By the time they came for me
There was no one left to even try.
Then they came for the pacifists
And they came for the priests
But I wasn't a pacifist
And I wasn't a priest
So I didn't stand up
And I didn't ask why
By the time they came for me
There was no one left to even try.
Then they came for the unionists

And they came for the gays
But I wasn't a unionist
And I wasn't gay

So I didn't stand up
And I didn't ask why
By the time they came for me
There was no one left to even try.
Now they come for the Muslims
And they come for the refugees
Though I am not a Muslim
And I'm not a refugee
Now I will stand up
And I will ask why
And when someday they come for me
I hope there's someone standing by my side.
Yes, we will stand up
Yes, we will ask why
And if someday they come for you
There'll be lots of people standing by your side
A world of people standing side by side.

To create socially just communities and classrooms in which all people are valued and safe, we have to work on many fronts. Teachers must take their responsibilities to create safe school environments very seriously, examining their curriculum, their pedagogy and the class-room climate. Headteachers and senior managers must support their teachers and staff so they make it clear that this is important and valued work within the school. And pupils can be encouraged to see themselves as powerful change agents within the school and the community. It is never too early or too soon to start making the world right.

References

Blue, B *'Courage,' Starting Small: songs for growing people ages 7-adult.* Bobblue.org (1990) Lyrics available at http://www.bobblue.org/pages/Song_Lyrics/Courage.html (accessed April 2008)

Henkes, K (1991) *Chrysanthemum.* New York: Greenwillow Press

Hoose, P and Hoose, H (1998) *Hey Little Ant.* Berkeley, CA: Tricycle Press

Moss, P (2004) *Say something.* Gardiner, Maine: Tilbury House

Niemöller, M. (1946) *First they came for the communists* (poem). Available at http://www.spartacus.schoolnet.co.uk/GERniemoller.htm (accessed April 2008)

Rosen, M and Graham, B (2005) *This Is My House*. Cambridge, MA: Candlewick Press

Sapon-Shevin, M (1999) B*ecause We Can Change the World: a practical guide to building cooperative, inclusive classroom communities.* Boston: Allyn and Bacon

Sapon-Shevin, M (2007) *Widening the circle: The power of inclusive classrooms.* Boston: Beacon Press

Stern, M 'Stand up,' *It's Nothing Fancy.* MikeSongs (2001) Lyrics available at http://www.lapointdesign.com/mikesongs/images.html (accessed April 2008)

11

Heads in the sand, backs against the wall: problems and priorities when tackling homophobia in schools

David Watkins

Echoing the recollections of Lesbian and Gay Youth Manchester and Frankham, Watkins reminds us that silence about sexuality can reinforce stereotypes and send powerful negative messages. A teacher in a school serving children with special needs, Watkins offers teachers with practical ideas on how to approach homosexuality in their classrooms. With examples and resources taken from successful lessons and anecdotal evidence from a staff group who have undergone training around LGB awareness, Watkins shows that there are creative and interesting ways to incorporate discussions about sexuality, and not just heterosexuality, into the curriculum. The approaches described here were used at Key Stage 3 and 4 with pupils with moderate learning difficulties but are also appropriate for primary level and can be extended for a secondary mainstream audience.

School – you'll never forget it

Jon: 'The only time that gay people were mentioned in sex education was when someone asked why I was a poof. The biology teacher explained that people were poofs because they were missing a chromosome' (Stonewall, 1993, p8).

Duncan: 'The boys would shout out to each other 'backs against the wall lads!' when I walked through the corridors. The only thing school taught me was what it felt like to be humiliated' (Stonewall, 1998, p40).

Teaching ignorance and fear does not achieve positive change. By refusing to deal appropriately with homosexuality, by ignoring or stigmatising it, their schools failed these pupils. Before the new millennium the government and schools themselves overlooked the importance of dealing with homosexuality in favour of tackling prejudices that were just as unacceptable but seemed to be more approachable, eg race and gender. In 2008 tackling religious hatred seems paramount. Worrying statistics show that a large number of schools are failing to provide specifically for the social and health education of lesbian, gay, bisexual and trans (LGBT) students. Tacitly implied within this breakdown is the failure to arm all students with the ability to negotiate the sexually diverse society in which they are growing up.

My aim in this chapter is to explore the issues surrounding homosexuality in special schools. Following the case study of good practice I look at the far-reaching effects of past homophobic legislation the effects of homophobic bullying. I give examples from my own teaching practice, how special and primary schools could be at the forefront of an LGBT-inclusive education, protection for LGBT staff and practical steps for all schools to provide for their LGBT population.

Case study: positive leadership

It is nearing the end of the summer term 2005 at a secondary special educational needs (SEN) school in Hampshire. Pupils aged 10 and 11 from the local feeder school are gathering for an induction assembly. Their journey through secondary school has the potential to be both exciting and challenging, but for some the journey may also be traumatic. Most are liable at some point to have been affected by homophobia and prejudice because of their perceived or actual sexuality.

'It is our aim to prevent that from happening here', says Janet, deputy headteacher, emphatically. 'At this school all children *and* staff are respected regardless of sexuality, age, gender, race, religion or disability.' Janet is keen to foreground sexuality in her statements. Her assembly makes plain the school's policy on homophobic bullying. Her stance is uncompromising. 'Bullying of any kind, including teasing because someone is Black, Indian, gay or disabled is unacceptable' she tells the children. Most children with moderate learning difficulties (MLD), some with severe learning difficulties (SLD) who are verbal, and primary school children will quickly pick up terminology which is offensive and use it pejoratively.

Janet reinforces the school's policy in a subsequent staff induction day, where she again states that 'bullying of *all kinds* is not tolerated. Homophobic bullying is a particular problem that we must be vigilant against.' With this in mind, the school's equal opportunities policy (EOP) has been updated since its inception at the opening of the school in 2003. I was asked to contribute to the policy when I first joined the staff as an unqualified teacher in 2004. Janet and I were optimistic and the school was open for change. Since then, the EOP has helped shape the school's behaviour policy and Physical and Social Development (PSD) statements. Here, on paper at least, there is the ability to deal with incidents of a homophobic nature and the freedom and support to deal with issues surrounding sexuality in the classroom. However, the assistant headteacher can still see areas for improvement.

Crafting an effective homophobic bullying policy is considered a point of focus by the inspectorate, Ofsted, not only for special schools but for all mainstream establishments. The difficulty in teaching in special schools is in adapting a high level secondary curriculum to children operating at a primary and reception level. All too often SEN teachers turn to a primary approach. Accordingly, it is vital that a foundation is laid about the seriousness of tackling inclusive issues no later than the primary level. Many SEN institutions have physically joined primary and secondary units, or maintain consistency between primary and secondary sites where the departments work in tandem to produce an inclusive ethos of diversity and respect. Later, I found such a school in Camden. It is clear that schools, in particular primary schools, need to facilitate this discussion if it is to be continued at the secondary level – but this hasn't always been the case. As Janet says, 'More needs to be done practically in schools and a review of anti-bullying and behaviour policy is currently underway. Staff need to be clear about what to do when they become aware of bullying.'

Heads in the sand

Up until 1998, Section 28 of the Local Government Act required Local Education Authorities not to 'promote the acceptability of homosexuality' and labelled gay relationships as 'pretend'. During these years, many teachers did not have the tools to tackle issues of homo-sexuality in schools, nor perhaps did they want to. But how can you tackle homophobic and transphobic bullying if you cannot discuss homosexuality? This homophobic clause created a climate of fear and panic and was mistakenly thought to apply directly to schools, making teachers wary of tackling any thing 'gay'. As a result many LGBT pupils were ignored, remained invisible, withdrew because of lack of support and experienced homophobic or transphobic bullying that was not appropriately dealt with. If we want to invest in children we need to invest in teachers. If teachers are receiving homophobic messages from school policies and senior leadership teams, how are these messages filtered down to the children?

> **Boy, Year 9**: 'The worst thing about homophobic bullying in my school is knowing that the teachers won't stop it' (DfES/DOH, 2004, p9).

It was estimated in 2004 that around '124,672 same-sex attracted pupils exist in mainstream maintained and independent secondary schools, [and of those] between 37,401 and 62,336 may have directly experienced homophobic bullying in England' (Warwick *et al*, 2004, p8). Homophobic insults are common in bullying incidents. Shying away from discussion about homosexuality can help fuel a culture of acceptance around homophobic bullying and set precedents for behaviour in adulthood. Homophobic bullying also destroys lives. According to Ian Rivers (2000), 50 percent of lesbian, gay and bisexual (LGB) students who had been bullied at school contemplated self-harm or suicide, and LGB pupils are more likely than their peers to leave school at 16.

These statistics are alarming, not least because they must only represent the tip of an iceberg. Childline estimated that 2,725 call each year to discuss sexual orientation or homophobic bullying (NSPCC, 2006). This culture of bullying does not arise suddenly out of nowhere in secondary school but has its roots in what is said and not said in primary schools.

Incidences of homophobic abuse and prejudice are often under-reported due to fears of pupils and staff facing recrimination or being outed. Although all pupils need to be able to talk about sexuality honestly, LGBT pupils may need extra support in school. These young people, like any minority group, will have to face discrimination in society. But for them, even home may offer no respite as a constructive place for their sexual identity, as their families may not accept their homosexuality. For some LGBT youth, school may be the one place where they can be themselves.

Teaching the importance of diversity

Young Man, 16: 'Teachers with street cred need to stand up for us; if you have respect for your teacher what they say is OK' (DfES/DOH, 2004, p3).

Though Section 28 was repealed in autumn 2002, its effects continued to cast a pall over how schools responded publicly to this emotive issue. Many teachers were unaware that they *did* have, and had always had, the power to affect change in their pupils' understanding of sexual diversity. The original purpose of Section 28 was misconstrued. It was never intended to apply directly to schools or teachers but to LEAs, which do not set Sex Education policy. Teachers now are on the front line in the new revolution of youth-centred LGBT awareness. Pupils, whether knowingly or not, look to them for advice and to model behaviour. LGBT youth lack role models to choose from. Schools need to explore examples of successful gays and lesbians that break down stereotypes and root the idea of sexuality as both incidental *and* complimentary to a person's success in life.

It is here where teachers who are out and comfortable with their sexuality play a crucial role in increasing LGBT visibility as lesbian and gay exemplars in children's lives. If pupils are protected from images of and proximity to real-life gay role models, for instance teachers and family friends, they will only have stereotypes and clouded prejudice from which to form their opinions. One pupil once said to me, 'It's good to know you can be gay and pretty cool, sir'. Respected gay and lesbian teachers who are out should never underestimate the powerful role they may have to play in the education of not just pupils but also whole staff groups. Some people might say that it is the duty of all LGBT teachers to come out, but this is a contentious issue and clouded by personal liberties.

Many teachers' contact with gay issues may stem from reactive strategies to homophobic bullying incidents. In order to tackle homophobia, schools and teachers need to develop proactive strategies that open

lines of communication to the realities of LGBT youth today and encourage an understanding and acceptance of LGBT relationships within the heterosexual population.

In a class of children aged 12 to 13, a pupil constantly used the term
'gay' to describe anything he didn't like. This use of the word as derogatory was unacceptable and I stopped the lesson. I had challenged his
use of the word privately and now I did so in front of the class, explaining my objections. This prompted a discussion about what was acceptable to say, which was further developed into a Personal and Social
Development (PSD) lesson. I asked the pupils to write down any words
they used or had heard used about someone who was gay. We talked
openly and honestly about words such as 'faggot', 'queer', 'poof', 'ponce',
'dyke', 'sissy boy', 'batty boy', 'gaylord', 'gay boy', 'lessie' and 'lesbo.'

So many of these words form part of a young person's vocabulary these
days. We discussed why there were so many negative words for homosexuality, and how it was closely linked with fear and hatred. We looked
at what images they evoked and why these words could be so harmful.
It was interesting to see that when the issues were laid open so frankly
and the words were no longer taboo in the context of the lesson, the
children felt able to have honest discussions examining their own prejudice. This discussion could equally well have happened in primary
classes of 8-10 year olds.

Of course, the use of the word 'gay' to mean anything that is without
value or substandard is now so prevalent in the vocabulary of children
even at a primary school that many teachers fail to challenge it because
they believe it has lost its negative connotation. Chris Moyles and BBC
Radio only further validated its use to a nation of young listeners when
in 2006 he described how a ring tone used on his show was rubbish and
therefore 'gay'. Language changes all the time, it is true, but this is not
simply the mutation of the adjective 'gay' that once defined something
that was 'bright and showy' or 'carefree'. The current use of the term is a
misuse of the definition for a community of people. Its use as a derogatory word is 'rooted in the idea that being gay is a bad thing which it is
acceptable to ridicule' (Schools OUT, 2006).

Would pupils' language remain as unchallenged if their vocabulary
changed to include use of the phrases 'don't be so Jewish' or 'this work

is so paki'? And how are LGBT pupils going to feel about their own sexuality if they constantly hear it referenced, whether homophobically or not, in such a negative way? As Claire Anderson of the Stamp Out Homophobia in Schools campaign, puts it, 'Victims of homophobic bullying will be made more vulnerable to abuse if there is any acceptance among staff or pupils that a derogatory use of 'gay' is not a homophobic attack' (Schools OUT, 2006).

Not all work has to take place in PSD or Citizenship lessons. Through drama and performing arts I have delivered a half term's work on bullying, running improvisation workshops that led to collaboration with a local Pupil Referral Unit (PRU) and the production of an anti-bullying DVD. I have challenged gender stereotypes, such as blue for a boy and pink for a girl, and have impressed upon my class the importance of individuality and uniqueness of thought and expression. This is particularly important for some boys due to the pressures of conforming to a masculine model that shuns feelings and empathy in favour of a hard, uncompromising gang culture. Challenging gender roles may also be the first step in unpicking homophobia.

Pink is now the fashionable colour in my class, especially on non-uniform days. Pupils vie with each other in class competitions to be on the pink team. One child even requested his Individual Educational Plan (IEP) targets to be printed on pink paper. These responses may appear trivial, but they represent seismic shifts in the thinking of teenage boys who at the start of term thought that men who liked pink were 'sissies' with 'a limp wrist'. Now, in this class there is demand for pink like never before. Blue is 'so last season'.

What do kids know?

I come from a background of special needs education, although I have witnessed homophobia in the mainstream first hand as a pupil in the 1990s and as a teacher in the new millennium. Is homophobia worse in the mainstream? Almost certainly yes, although homophobic attitudes amongst staff can be found in both settings. Much of this chapter is based on my experience as a teacher in a special school, but recently in 2006 I spent twelve weeks in a mainstream environment and found homophobia amongst pupils there to be weakly tolerated and almost always tacitly permissible.

There was the ubiquitous almost constant use of the word 'gay' to represent things without value and the failure or inability amongst staff to challenge it. But in this mainstream setting I observed homophobic activity to be particularly pronounced amongst 11 to 14 year-old boys. They would hurl homophobic insults at their teacher or other pupils anywhere and in any way that befitted the setting, eg whispering and joking in lessons, calling out in the playground and voicing insults loudly and clearly behind people's backs in corridors or under their breath through doorways. Homophobia seemed even more widespread than I had remembered as a teenager in school fifteen years ago. Significantly, this school made no mention of LGBT rights in any policy and no clear sanctions to deal with homophobic bullying. The few teachers who did take a stand and wrote negative referrals reported that senior leaders treated these referrals as minor infractions and pupils were simply told not to do it again.

I myself found it increasingly hard to challenge the behaviour I witnessed around me. The word 'gay' seemed at times to ricochet around the classroom and I was never 100 percent sure who the perpetrators were. I found it difficult to make time to explain to these children one-on-one what they had done wrong and why their behaviour was unacceptable. With 150 children passing through the classroom each day and no learning support assistant, I had neither the time nor resources to offer these children extended dialogue that challenged their homophobia or tried to redress it, something I was able to do in a special school setup.

No sex, please, we're British

I have encountered some resistance to the idea that children with SEN should be allowed access to ideas surrounding diverse sexual orientations. There is the palpable fear, vociferously voiced by a headteacher I once worked for, that children with SEN cannot 'cognitively process what is means to be gay', and therefore either do not need to know more than the essentials of (straight) sex or have no right to a sexuality themselves. So-called educators like these see children with SEN as devoid of sexuality, unable to recognise their basic human needs for feelings of love and the desire for companionship or intimacy. There is need for further analysis of a field which has been all too neglected in recognising people with disabilities and their sexualities, including their current and future biological and emotional needs for love and sexual expression. In my experience children with special needs, even 13 year-old boys who are socially savvy, are more able than their mainstream counterparts to accept the concept of different sexualities and the need to grant gays and lesbians the same rights as the rest of the community.

Most importantly, children with special needs know what it is like to be discriminated against; they are often bullied in mainstream schools or by their peers where they live and they can identify more readily with the fallout of prejudice and marginalisation. For children in special schools there is no behavioural norm so they are more likely to accept difference in others. For some boys with moderate to severe learning difficulties there is less pressure or expectation on them to live up to the stereotype of a masculine male identity or role in society as their special needs can sometimes exclude them from traditional routes through life that other children would take for granted, such as sexual experimentation, girlfriends, marriage and so on. It must be stressed, however, that many children with special needs can be particularly vulnerable in the sexual world because of their learning difficulties.

Certainly among the boys aged 12 to 13 in the special school there was little resistance to discussing the notion of homosexuality, perhaps because there was less pressure for them to pair off with a girl or to prove or demonstrate masculine qualities amongst their peer group. I believe homophobia has roots in the traditional understanding of the male and female roles in society. Gays and lesbians who cross gender roles and subvert so-called normal gender behaviour can be seen as threatening to teenagers who need these straight stereotypes to create a sexual identity as they develop. Looking at the prescriptive assignation of masculine and feminine roles to boys and girls may help us understand how homosexuality can threaten these gender roles and lead to homophobia. Changing how we educate children around sexism and issues of gender may therefore be key in unlocking their potential to assimilate the concept of homosexuality at an early age.

There is still a simmering fear in education that wants to hide the full diversity of sexuality from even mainstream children. This is the same misguided fear that associates gay men with paedophiles and assumes that talking about homosexuality encourages young children to experiment and maybe even turns them gay. Sexuality, a loaded and sometimes misleading word, has that danger word SEX within, but in reality sexuality doesn't revolve simply around sex but rather sexual identity, love, empathy, kinship and comfort: things we all need and search for. Sexuality brings about life and it makes life worth living. Sexuality affects us all.

Contrary to what some parents and educators may think, sexuality is as important to young people as it is to adults. Shying away from discussing these issues in the classroom means that pupils will glean misinformation from their friends and a homophobic society. Young people are already talking about sexuality in the playground and learning from the media. They need a safe environment in which they can ask questions about sex and know they will get an honest answer. Staff must, of course, be sensitive about the time and place for such discussion and any sensitivities within the group.

Protection for staff

Staff need to come together to form a whole-school approach. Pupils may receive mixed messages if one staff member raises awareness of homophobia whilst another lets homophobic insults slide. This only serves to promote an us and them binary, where students pit teachers who are perceived as pro-gay, whom they see as nagging and uptight about homophobic language, against their more laid-back colleagues who passively condone homophobic behaviour by their silence. These pro-gay teachers may be targeted as gay themselves and suffer homophobia from students if they are not supported by the entire school group, including governors. Ultimately, the question schools need to ask themselves is: What does tackling homophobia mean for staff training and support?

Note that schools can fall into the trap of assuming that only their LGBT staff are suitably equipped to deliver PSD lessons on homosexuality or tackle issues of homophobic bullying. It is sometimes these teachers who find it most difficult to talk openly about homosexuality, if perhaps for fear of being outed or facing recrimination from pupils and staff alike.

In many job sectors, employees would not expect to come to work to face an abundance of unchallenged homophobic abuse. Why should they have to tolerate this simply because they are working with children? We must expect that schools fall into line with the ethos of a modern-day work place, and that means protection for all staff. Employment laws passed on December 1, 2003 have made it illegal for employers to discriminate against an employee based upon the grounds of perceived or actual sexual orientation. But many teachers, gay and straight, have not been advised of the new legislation, or of the repeal of Section 28. As well as giving gay pupils the protection and support they need at school, the removal of Section 28 can benefit the corporate life of schools.

Sue Sanders of the LGBT training and lobby group Schools OUT points out the financial benefits for headteachers taking the lead, 'Treating all employees with respect and consideration also helps a school recruit and retain their best staff ... this could now also preserve their reputation, as it's less likely they'd be hauled up in front of tribunals under these new laws' (Anon, 2004). In February 2008, I took a homophobic headteacher and governors of a school to tribunal under the Sexual Orientation Regulations 2003, and won, becoming to my knowledge, the first teacher in the UK to do so.

Raising awareness

February 2006 was the first LGBT History Month at my secondary special educational needs school in Hampshire. This programme aims to provide cultural awareness of gay and lesbian historical contributions to society. Flagging and positioning the work of many lesbians and gay men throughout history can help pupils begin to see the benefits of an inclusive society where contributions from everybody are valid. The idea from Schools OUT, set up in February 2005, gained support from MP Jacqui Smith, who wrote in an email to LGBT networks, 'I believe the month will be important in helping to drive the culture change to create a more inclusive society' (2004).

Facing the front

In 2004, an article in *Teachers' Magazine* outlined some proactive steps to an inclusive school. These included:

- use e-mail filters that don't block LGBT-related words
- advertise for recruits in LGBT media and include explicit EOP/ inclusion statements in all adverts and application packs; deliver LGBT diversity training in all staff inductions
- review support procedures for LGBT staff who wish to come out (Anon, 2004)

Through research and through personal experience I have compiled a list of my own practical steps for a LGBT friendly school:

- Review all practices and policies, including equal opportunities policy (EOP) and anti-bullying policy
- Adopt a whole-school zero-tolerance approach to homophobic bullying with effective sanctions
- Be vigilant in and out of class about the use of homophobic language
- Don't be heterosexist – that is, assume that everyone is heterosexual. Using the non-gender specific term 'partner' is a good way to bring together all sexualities in discussion of relationships
- Create a homophobic report log and log incidents in ABC charts using codes which show bullying incidents at a glance, eg 'R' for racism, 'S' for sexism, and 'H' for homophobia.
- Promote positive images in class that challenge queer stereotypes. Make sure wall displays are inclusive. Showing a picture of two men kissing on the lips is not gratuitous, though for some it may prove uncomfortable, just as interracial kisses once did. Understand that LGBT people intersect all equal rights. LGBT people are old, young, male, female, Asian, Black, White, differently abled, and from all faiths and religions. Reflect this in your teaching of the world.

Schools in motion

Although this chapter is based largely on secondary special school experience, educating children about sexuality should start in primary school. I know from experience in primary schools that the issues are the same. Young children, like many of the SEN kids I have worked with, are not yet programmed with homophobia. We shouldn't be afraid of talking to young children about being gay. Teaching diverse sexual identities at Key Stage 1and 2 means showing strong clear positive images and recognising that for some children the word 'family' can mean something quite different to the perceived norm of one mother and one father.

It means talking about love in all its manifestations. It means looking at the festivals of all communities in Geography, Religious Education and Citizenship, not just those of race or religion, but also the pride parades and street fairs, the special days of so many gays and lesbians in so many countries. If this means promoting homosexuality as a valid family relationship, then why not? What is wrong with promoting homosexuality in the context of loving relationships? Surely a society that emphasises honesty and love is better than one that emphasises any and all heterosexual relationships, even if they are marred by divorce, violence or resentment.

Contrary to the now defunct Section 28, I as a teacher am engaged in promotion all the time. Teachers promote respect, diversity and compassion. Teachers promote celebrations, faiths, ethnicities, and the values of different cultures. As much as a school may promote the cultural diversity of Islam by looking at Muslim families and festivals such as Ramadan and Eid and examining examples of Muslim culture, schools should be promoting gay communities and their values by celebrating gay symbols, relationships, and contributions across the world.

Talking, really talking, and educating people about homosexuality isn't just a matter of showing more than stereotypes or destroying perverted notions of homosexuality. It isn't only about empowering teachers to stamp out homophobic bullying. If we cannot talk about homosexuality, we cannot fully educate our future society.

Throughout this chapter, I have shown why homophobia in schools is a problem and why addressing it should be a priority. Homophobia, like all forms of prejudice, is something that is learned, not innate. As major educators in a child's life, it is vital that schools organise themselves to teach diversity and acceptance – and the earlier, the better. With every generation we have the opportunity for a more positive future. Surely that's the aim of all schools: to help create a better world? Children are a dynamic force. Teachers and schools with their backs to the wall and heads in the sand create a world without movement, a world in which little can change. This homophobia comes from the adult world, not a child's, and is a homophobia that schools have a duty to counteract. To create a more diverse and tolerant society, children's inherent acceptance of difference needs to be harnessed as early as primary or even infant school. Sadly, for the boys quoted at the start of this chapter and their classmates, it may already be too late. But for the children starting school now, today, there will never be a better time. There has been no space here to examine in detail the needs of transgender or intersex pupils but the conclusions I might reach about their equality and needs in education would surely remain consistent with my opinions on LGB students. Honest educators encourage children to find their own identity and self-acceptance and if they find the answers, then these are the best qualifications they can take from school.

References

Anonymous (2004) Tackling homophobia *Teachers' Magazine* 33 (July) http://www. teachernet.gov.uk/teachers/issue33/secondary/features/Tacklinghomophobia_Secon dary/ (December 2005)

Department for Education and Skills and Department of Health (2004) *Stand up for Us: Challenging Homophobia in Schools.* London: Department for Education and Skills and Department of Health

NSPCC (2006) Calls to Childline about sexual orientation, homophobia, and homophobic bullying. http://www.nspcc.org.uk/Inform/publications/Serials/ChildLine Casenotes/CLcasenotessexualorientation_wdf48181.pdf (May 2008)

Rivers, I (2000) Social exclusion, absenteeism and sexual minority youth. *Support for Learning* 15(1) p13-18

Smith, Jacqui (2004) Email correspondence http://www.schools-out.org.uk/ news/archive2004/jacquismithletter.htm (May 2008)

Schools OUT (2006) Press release: BBC says use of the word 'gay' in a derogatory manner is not offensive! http://www.schools-out.org.uk/ (May 2008)

Stonewall (1993) *Arrested Development: Stonewall Survey on the Age of Consent and Sex Education.* London: Stonewall

Stonewall (1998) Arrested development: Stonewall survey on the age of consent and sex education. In Donnellan, C (Ed) *Homosexuality (Issues).* Cambridge: Independence Educational Publishers

Warwick, I., Chase, E, Aggleton, P, w/Sanders, S (2004) *Homophobia, Sexual Orientation and Schools: a Review and Implications for Action.* London: Department for Education and Skills/University of London

12

Exploring gender identity, queering heteronormativity

Renée DePalma and Elizabeth Atkinson

In this chapter, DePalma and Atkinson demonstrate how sex/gender/ sexuality processes are conflated in society and schools. While sexual identity, gender performance and sexuality are actually very different aspects of human experiences, they become closely entangled in a heterosexual matrix of assumptions and socially-constructed relationships. Based on data emerging from the *No Outsiders* project as well as earlier research involving interviews with primary teachers and trainees, the authors analyse how both adults and young children experience and express systematic heteronormativity by conflating gender conformity and sexuality and how the cultural resources available to children and adults reinforce this process. Building on the practical approaches offered by Hinton, Sapon-Shevin and Watkins, DePalma and Atkinson argue that Queer Theory, an understanding based on troubling normative categories and raising (and holding) fundamental questions, can help us to understand and challenge heteronormative processes in schools.

Children, society and popular culture: conflating sex/gender/sexuality

Popular notions of childhood tend to construct children to be somehow innocent of assumptions about sexuality (Renold, 2005), but others argue that children are in fact constantly bombarded with messages that propagate the heterosexual matrix, which Butler defines as:

that grid of cultural intelligibility through which bodies, genders, and desires are naturalized ... a hegemonic discursive/epistemological model of gender intelligibility that assumes that for bodies to cohere and make sense there must be a stable sex expressed through a stable gender (masculine expresses male, feminine expresses female). (1990, p 151)

Linné's reading of the popular Disney film *The Lion King* (Walt Disney Feature Animation, 1994) highlights the ways in which sex and gender norms (and the threat of their transgressions) underpin the basic narrative:

The 'circle of life' is threatened when the Lion King's effete, purple eye-shadow-wearing brother Scar usurps the crown through conniving and murder. In the hands of this childless, queer loner the kingdom sinks into a dark age of decadence and evil. Only when the patriarchy is restored via the young male prince and his helpmate bride does moral order and prosperity return to the savannah. (2003, p673)

Scar's gender queer demeanour provides an entertaining and believable backdrop to his challenge to the patriarchal order, drawing upon our implicit association of gender and sexual transgression to create a familiarly evil and threatening character. Disney did not create sex/gender conflation, but draws upon it artistically, playing upon existing associations and, in so doing, reinforcing and quietly perpetuating them.

This sex/gender conflation is reflected not only in popular media, but in society's reactions to it. Consider the public response to Tinky Winky, the universally recognised and either vilified or adored 'gay Teletubby'. Recently officials in Poland have accused Tinky Winky of promoting a homosexual lifestyle by carrying a 'woman's' red handbag (Easton, 2007). Journalist Michael Colton, whose article in the style section of the *Washington Post* helped to create the Teletubby's status as a gay icon, later reflected on his reasons for playfully 'outing' Tinky Winky, 'Tinky Winky is obviously not homosexual[1], by any stretch of the imagination, but he possesses a few effeminate characteristics (he also likes to wear a tutu on occasion)' (1999). Nevertheless, Tinky Winky had only to flout gender norms by wearing 'women's' accessories to earn a worldwide reputation as sexually transgressive and, according to US televangelist Jerry Falwell, threatening to children.

The children's book *The Sissy Duckling* (Fierstein and Cole, 2002) has come under similar fire in both the US and the UK for depicting a 'gay' duckling, despite the fact that there are no clues to the duckling's sexuality aside from his tendency to dance around the forest home wearing a pink apron and carrying a feather duster. Whether or not Fierstein, an openly gay artist and gay activist, imagined gay romance to be in Elmer's future, he has provided readers with only Elmer's gender transgressions as evidence[2]. This seems to have even further enraged religious conservatives, who read the lack of an explicitly gay theme to be an act of subterfuge:

> *The Sissy Duckling* should be a wake-up call for evangelicals. Conservative Christians were outraged a few years ago by books such as *Daddy's Roommate* and *Heather Has Two Mommies*. But, those volumes were upfront about their homosexual agenda. Books such as *The Sissy Duckling* are subtler, and thus even more dangerous for vulnerable and confused kids. (Moore, 2007)

In the UK, the Christian Institute (2006) published a document criticising the government's recommended resources on homosexuality for schools,[3] which includes *The Sissy Duckling*. The other four resources targeted in this critique feature homosexual relationships. While the Christian Institute does not explicitly attack Elmer for being a 'gay' duckling, the inclusion of this book as a 'recommended resource on homosexuality' suggests an unconscious and automatic conflation of sexuality/gender.

We do not mean to imply that this conflation is an affliction suffered by the homophobic, or even the heterosexual; one lesbian reviewer positively describes Elmer as 'your *stereotypical gay boy* duckling: helpful around the house, he likes to paint pictures, put on puppet shows and decorate cookies' (Beckett, 2007, our emphasis). It may well be that Fierstein plays consciously upon the discourses available to us to construct a gay ducking without explicitly using sexuality cues; the question is not whether or not Elmer is a gay duckling, but that it is almost impossible to read him as otherwise given the degree to which discursive cues as to gender and sexuality signify one another for most informed readers.

These examples demonstrate how the heterosexual matrix works to create stereotypes by conflating sex/gender/sexuality: in the absence of a physical human body, Teletubbies are assigned sex based on voice and perhaps convention, that is, male unless clearly signalled otherwise, but a 'woman's' handbag clearly marks 'him' as a gay man. Elmer is identified as a stereotypically gay duckling because he performs girl in terms of behaviour and hobbies.

Conflating sex/gender/sexuality in classrooms: Heteronormativity goes to school

From September 2005 to August 2006 we conducted in-depth interviews with 72 practising and prospective primary teachers and teacher trainees across the UK to develop a better understanding of how the heterosexual matrix works in primary schools. One aspect we wanted to explore was how the kinds of socially constructed sex/gender/sexuality conflations described above might operate in schools to define and limit even very young children's possibilities by constructing a limited number of comprehensible and co-varying categories. We were interested to explore whether sexuality was elided with gender performances. That is, were assumptions about sexuality formed on the basis of gendered performances, as in the case of the flaming Tinky Winky and Elmer as the stereotypically gay ducking?

Interviewees were asked to describe any gender-non-conforming children they had come in contact with and the reactions of peers and teachers. These responses formed a theme of sex/gender/sexuality conflation: transgressing any of these socially defined categories tended to trouble others. One particular instance involved a 10 year-old girl who was described as 'confused' because she 'wanted to be treated like a boy, and looks like a boy and wants to act like a boy. But has been very upset obviously when people have mistaken her for a boy. And have referred to her as a boy.' This girl seems to have demanded a distinction between sex (she is a girl) and gender (she wants to do boy), yet perhaps it is exactly her refusal to collude sex/gender in the usual way that results in her being described as confused. While the girl had apparently not made any claims about her sexuality, her mother's concerns seemed to centre on sexuality, 'Her mum said to me quite specifically that she didn't want her to be gay when she grew up, because she wouldn't be able to have children and they didn't approve of that sort of thing in their house.' The teacher's reflection reveals her own assumptions in terms of sexuality, 'I don't know whether she wants to be a boy or she just doesn't want to be girly ... There's a difference between, you know, being tomboyish and deciding that you're actually gay, you know ... at this age for them to know that difference is very hard.' While ostensibly insisting on separating tomboy behaviour and a lesbian identity, the suggestion that the girl is too young to know whether she is gay reveals an implicit connection: she will eventually have to decide whether she is simply a tomboy or an *actual* lesbian, as if the two were different places on the same spectrum.

We found more instances of gender-sexuality entanglement for boys than girls: boys as young as 5 and 6 were being read as proto-gay for their gendered transgressions. These included carrying a pink lunch box, playing in the home corner, refusing to play rough sports and opting to read or play fantasy games. These instances reinforce Butler's notion that performing unintelligible gender is connected with unintelligible sexualities. One teacher, for example, paraphrased colleagues' comments on a reception-aged (4-5) boy who spent rather a lot of time playing with girls and the toys and games usually associated with them, 'Oh he's obviously gay. He's got to be gay. He's going to be gay when he grows up. It's just so obvious.'

Another teacher, a gay man, said he identified children who might grow up to be gay by looking for characteristics that he himself displayed as a child:

> Being more of an outsider, being more of a loner. And sort of, not particularly liking sports, being more of a reader and just, just the ways that they behave, being more effeminate than their peers. That's how they've kind of stood out for me.

The interesting thing for us was that we recognised what he said. It resonated with the connections we tend to make ourselves and the theme that ran all through the teachers' interviews. As we listened to the teachers' stories and recognised our own assumptions in what they reported, we realised that any research involving queering schools would have to include an interrogation of our own heteronormative understandings.

Very young children may themselves appropriate sex/gender/sexuality conflations as they struggle to define themselves in terms that adults understand. One teacher spoke of a Year 2 (age 6 or 7) boy who explicitly described himself in terms of sexuality, 'He says, 'I'm gay, I like boys.'' But from her own interactions with the boy and the reports of other teachers she could not recall any indication that he had expressed or demonstrated a particular attraction to boys. In fact, she remembered that he expressed and acted upon a particular fondness for touching women's breasts. He also described himself as a 'tomgirl' and, when asked to explain, he based his description on his preference for stereotypically girl behaviours, 'I don't like football, I like mermaids, I like the colour pink...' The teacher suggested that he had appropriated the term 'gay' as well as 'tomboy' (which he transformed into 'tomgirl') to explain his own gender transgressions.

Another theme that emerged from these interviews was that while many teachers could recall instances of children comfortably transgressing gender stereotypes when very young – from nursery up to about 7 years old – few teachers remembered such transgressions occurring in the later primary years. When older children did transgress gender norms, teachers reported discomfort among teachers and parents. One teacher reminisced about a Year 2 boy in her previous school who was 'particularly fond of a rather flamboyant feather boa, which got in the way in playing football'. She recalled a general air of acceptance for the way this boy happily blurred gender lines, but predicted that had she stayed on she would have seen a change: 'At that age a child doing something like that is read perhaps differently than if he had been 9 and doing it'.

One headteacher described how the taboo against gender transgressions that inhibited children's behaviours became stronger as they got older, 'You know, I can walk into foundation stage [ages 3-5] classrooms and I can see the boys bathing the babies and you know, that's fantastic, but as I go up to Years 4, 5 and 6 [ages 8-11] ... it's a learnt taboo.' Some teachers described how peer pressures enforced this taboo and how they tended to draw upon a homophobic discourse to enforce gender norms, 'Boys who cry when they get hurt might be called 'wuss,' 'sissy,' 'girl' or 'gay.'' As one headteacher pointed out, the associations between gender and sexuality can be used strategically, 'A group of 8 and 9 year-old girls were calling a boy 'gay' ... they were trying to position him as quite effeminate, as quite weak, all those sort of negative connotations.'

This kind of strategic conflation of sex/gender/sexuality fits Suzanne Pharr's characterisation of homophobia as a weapon of sexism:

> A lesbian is perceived as a threat to the nuclear family, to male dominance and control, to the very heart of sexism ... misogyny gets transferred to gay men with a vengeance and is increased by the fear that their sexual identity and behaviour will bring down the entire system of male dominance and compulsory heterosexuality. (1988, p18-19)

As Pharr points out, transgressing sexual norms evokes fear and anger that gender norms have been transgressed as well, and the easy conflation of sex/gender/sexuality allows homophobia and misogyny to work hand in hand to castigate those who transgress any category defined by the heterosexual matrix. Our research suggests that the way schools are structurally organised reinforces the construction and conflation of sex/gender/sexuality categories and polices their transgressions. Everything from boys' and girls' sports to the division of play areas (home corner vs. construction) provides an ideal backdrop for policing the heterosexual matrix, as children's gendered play choices seem to be especially salient in producing assumptions about sexual identity and sexuality.

This conflation of sex, gender and sexuality ignores the fact that these are in reality separate aspects of human identity and experience. One might do gender in a variety of ways in terms of dress, behaviour, movement, gesture, speech, etc. One might explicitly claim a gendered identity, or refuse to take one on at all. A person's gendered performance may or may not reflect what we take to be that person's biological sex, so that a young girl may choose to wear a 'boy's' school uniform, or an adult woman may have a penis. This young girl and this woman, furthermore, may consider themselves and call themselves girl or boy, man or woman. One's gender and sex does not predict sexual orientation. So a quiet boy who likes to read and play in the dressing up corner is not necessarily going to be attracted to other boys, and the girl who refuses to wear dresses will not necessarily come to identify as lesbian. It is difficult not to elide these categories, drawing upon evidence from one category (wearing dresses or trousers or feather boas) as evidence for another (desiring boys or girls). These are the kinds of assumptions we explore in this chapter. What do these sex/gender/sexuality elisions look like in primary schools, where do they come from and what kind of thinking and action will it take to undo them?

Toward queering early childhood education: an action research project interrogating heteronormativity in primary schools

Nearly ten years have passed since Letts and Sears challenged teachers to queer elementary education, 'Teaching queerly demands we explore taken for granted assumptions ... to deconstruct these sexual and gender binaries (deployed and reified through social text and grammar) that are the linchpins of heteronormativity' (1999, p5-6). But can schools themselves, places where we tend to seek answers rather than questions, be sites for this kind of interrogation?

Our own current research in UK primary schools seeks both to identify ways in which primary schools propagate the heterosexual matrix and ways to queer these heteronormative processes. In a two-year collaborative participatory action research project called *No Outsiders,* teachers and university researchers have been using feminist, post-structuralist and queer theory perspectives to explore and deconstruct what Butler defines as the heterosexual matrix. Project members are based in primary schools throughout the UK and communicate with each other through a web-based discussion forum where field notes and other data are also shared among team members. Data emerging in the first year of the project (2006-2007) has yielded interesting insights into the nature of gender and sexuality norms and how they are conflated within early years educational settings.

Field notes written by a headteacher in the project reveals the extent to which gender roles are reinforced through family and society. She recalls the reaction of the parents of 4 year-olds to her suggestion that not only girls but also boys might wish to transgress gendered clothing norms:

> Our experienced, indeed veteran, reception teacher [says], 'Boys can wear grey trousers, girls can wear a little grey skirt or a pinafore dress. Sometimes,

because they haven't got much of a waist at this age, skirts can be difficult.' The teacher moves on to another topic altogether. I interrupt, 'Of course girls can also wear grey trousers, too...' and pause (and everyone takes this as a reasonable addition to the information already given), then as an after-thought, 'and boys can wear skirts if they wish.' Everyone laughs.

Conscious that she had purposely evoked the reaction she had expected, the headteacher reflected on what the results of her micro-experiment revealed about ingrained societal understandings:

These are the parents of 4 year-olds ... but already we have determined that it would be strange/odd/ laughable if the boys dressed in skirts/tights. We are so stacking up trouble for ourselves in years to come, don't you think?

Another project teacher's field notes reveal a fascinating discussion inspired by reading the poem *Gender Pretender* by Benjamin Zephaniah (2002) with her 8 and 9 year-old pupils. The teacher reflects on the children's strong understandings of what is and is not allowable in terms of gender and sexuality:

They said that it would be fine for a boy to dress up like a princess but then were beginning to say that actually a boy would get teased more for dressing like that than a girl would for wearing boys' clothes. One child said that every-one would think a boy was gay if they did that. So that got us talking ... The boys in the group, especially, were saying 'it's nasty', 'two men or two girls kissing is gross', 'it's not normal'. When I asked why they thought it's not normal, they said that 'you don't see people doing it.' They also said that boys have to wear girls' clothes to kiss each other and that girls have to dress up as boys if they want to kiss each other and that if two gay people get married, one has to dress up as a woman so people won't find out.

— This discussion also revealed how gender and sexuality are inextricably
— intermingled within the heterosexual matrix, to the extent that trans-gressing sexuality norms (boys kissing boys, men marrying men) re-quired transgressing gender norms (boys dressing as girls).

Our *No Outsiders* research attempts to answer the question posed earlier, 'What would teaching queerly look like?' We think that it begins with the kind of critical interrogation of our schools and ourselves des-cribed above. This means uncovering the implicit assumptions that make parents laugh at the prospect of 4 year-old boys wearing dresses and that suggest to children that boys should wear dresses to kiss each other. It also means uncovering our own assumptions and developing a questioning stance in an environment where answers are highly valued. This does not necessarily mean never having *any* answers, but rather a sort of strategic uncertainty that allows us to trouble hegemonic certainties, such as the sex/gender/sexuality categories and conflations that make up the heterosexual matrix. What if boys wore dresses to school? Let us just imagine that for a moment...

Sue, the *No Outsiders* teacher who raised this particular question for parents, is headteacher of a small village church school. A principle central to her philosophy of teaching is what she describes as 'holding the question'. She states, 'I believe holding the question is the key to learning – it's where the deep learning takes place. Some teachers and children think that it's the answers that matter, but it's not.' While Sue professes to be completely baffled by the discussions some of the *No Outsiders* university researchers have about Queer Theory, we read Sue's desire to 'hold the question' as a queering technique. Recently one of us wrote to her to explain why:

> Because you resist the temptation to rush to certainty, find clear answers to everything. You allow for, recognise and work with uncertainties. This relates for example to the notion of queering that we use a lot, which means that it is very useful to just shake up people's notions of what is normal: challenging assumptions about what goes together ... and what doesn't go together ... But it's not *just* about living with, exploring and working with uncertainties, it's about social justice in the end. There's some debate about whether uncertainty is helpful in the pursuit of justice, and I would say yes. Others would say no. So your interest in 'holding the question' suggests that at least to some extent you agree with me. (Renée, first author, to Sue on the project web discussion forum, 4 July, 2007)

This insistence on holding the question has allowed Sue to strategically bring uncertainty into pedagogic contexts that are more likely to entail seeking answers. We do not, however, claim that this is an easy stance to maintain, and exploring our own struggles with tendencies to resort to the heterosexual matrix of easy categories and conflations is a crucial part of our *No Outsiders* project work.

It is perhaps the difficulty of holding the question which makes the non-normative gender performance of one 6 year-old child in Sue's school troublesome to the researcher as well as his peers. Neville has expressed a great desire to play the part of the fairy godmother in a pantomime production of *King and King* (De Haan and Nijland, 2002), a tale in which two princes fall in love, and Neville's wish has been granted. The pantomime is to be performed at the village church and later for a special inclusion ceremony off school grounds, but during preparations Neville's performance of his newly-acquired gender role causes some of the girls in his class some consternation. The following reflective observations were conducted by Elizabeth, second author, at Sue's school and are recorded by Elizabeth in the first person. Below are two extracts from her field notes:

Now we're in the hall and, without my noticing, Neville has been dressed in his white satin dress (with added bosom), blonde wig and sparkling wand. He comes over to me.

Neville: What do you think of this? I'm the fairy godmother and I've got a bosom.

Another boy: He's the fairy godmother and he's got boobs – he's got pretend boobies.

Elizabeth (researcher): Well, I assumed that they were pretend!

Same boy: He's got a wig. (Reaches out and grabs it; Neville backs off and straightens it, and a girl standing nearby fixes on his pink feather and diamanté tiara.)

Neville: Are you coming up to the – um- the church? I might use a bit of a different voice – I won't use my usual boy voice.

A little later, I look across the floor: Neville is now bashing the wide-brimmed hat off another boy with his wand.

Later in the rehearsal, Neville flounces over to me with pursed lips, wafting his wand. He giggles and whispers, 'Hmhm – this is very good, isn't it!' I nod and smile.

At the afternoon performance in the village church, another researcher tells me that two girls have been talking to her, talking about Neville and another boy, both of whom have transgressed gender lines for this performance, 'He's got boobies – and so has Neville – and he's got a wig, and we've been talking about it at lunchtime and we think he looks like a girl.'

The following Monday, headteacher Sue tells me that Neville doesn't want to come to perform the role of the fairy godmother at an out-of-school event at which the school is being presented with an inclusion award. (Elizabeth's observational field note)

As it happened, Neville did appear and play his part at the inclusion award ceremony; but in the context of this analysis it is the effect on his female peers that is especially interesting. What is perhaps particularly disturbing for the girls is that he is taking it completely seriously. He is not once observed to laugh *about* his role – the giggle as he comes up to me is one of pleasure, not of parody, and the pursed lips appear more for his own pleasure than for others' observation. None of his actions or words suggest the sort of exaggeration that implies either em-barrassment or ridicule. Nothing in his performance – whether on stage or between acts, suggests that Neville sees this as parody or subversion: he is not doing drag, with all the connotations that that brings. He is simply being the fairy godmother. For the female onlookers, perhaps Neville's body has become an impossible body (Youdell, 2006).

Without parody, this boy-girl is altogether too disturbing for his peers' comfort. *He looks like a girl* has significantly different connotations from *he is acting like a girl* – and indeed, Elizabeth reflected later that had she not known that it was Neville inside the dress and the wig, she might easily have taken him for a girl all along. His repetition of the echo-chains of feminine gendered performativity is subversive *only* if we know that he happens to be boy, and that this costume breaks the current dress code for boys of his age. Had he belonged to the wealthier classes in England a century or more ago, he would have been dressed in frocks in his early childhood. By omitting parody from his perfor-mance – by just being a boy-in-a-dress – Neville is confounding his on-lookers' sense of *why* he is taking on the performance at all. And by *not* using parody in his gendered performance, perhaps Neville himself is inadvertently engaged in an act of queering.

The sex/gender/sexuality conflations invoked and challenged by Neville's act of gender queering became apparent when Elizabeth joined Neville and his father and younger brother at the awards cere-mony a few days later. In her field notes she reflected on ways in which he brought to the surface some of her own implicit assumptions about gender and sexuality:

As I sit with Neville at the round table with his father and his younger brother, Neville suddenly catches sight of my *No Outsiders* pen, with its logo: No Outsiders: Challenging homophobia in primary schools. Slowly but surely, he begins to sound out the words on the pen. *No Outsiders* is fine – but as he gets closer and closer to homophobia my heart starts to race . . . what if he asks what it means? What will I say? What will his father say? To my relief, he sounds it out incorrectly, doesn't ask for an interpretation, moves on to *in primary schools* then turns his attention to something else. (Elizabeth, observational field notes)

Later, Elizabeth thought back on her field observations in her reflection journal and analysed the source of her discomfort at Neville's performance and her later encounter with him and his father:

My consternation during this incident arises from two sources. Firstly, my fear is that if I have to explain to Neville what 'homophobia' means, he will realise that because he is choosing to wear a dress, I am assuming he is going to grow up gay. And secondly, and worse, I realise with a slow shock that I have caught myself in the act of making the very assumption which continually reconstitutes the heterosexual matrix: I am assuming that he will grow up gay purely because he is not 'doing boy' (Renold, 2005, 2006) according to established gender norms. I recall the moment during the rehearsal when Neville used his magic wand to knock another character's hat off his head, and I recall, too, my feeling of disturbance at this: a feeling that he was somehow betraying me – or betraying my delight in his girl-ness – by 'doing boy' wearing his dress. Once again, perhaps, Neville is inadvertently engaged in an act of queering: without knowing it, he is reminding me that boys in dresses and girls in trousers might both poke hats off the heads of other children – and that has absolutely nothing to do with their sexual orientation! (Elizabeth, journal reflection)

These observations and reflections gave Elizabeth a chance to investigate the processes of heteronormativity and queering at work in a primary school, her own implication in these processes included. While Sue's pantomime production of *King and King* (with a fairy godmother added, played by a boy) raised and opened questions for Elizabeth as well as the other participants and spectators, Elizabeth's conscious participation in a queering project inspired her to interrogate her own tendency to define categories, make connections and close down the open questions.

Pedagogically speaking, the question driving *No Outsiders* is how to teach queerly, that is, how to plan for and support opportunities for questioning the heteronormative. Queering seems to be an indirect thing: rather than seek out the definitive queer curriculum, the *No Outsiders* project looks for ways that queer moments might arise in the classroom. As Sue's pantomime performance based on *King and King* illustrated, we have found creative arts such as literature and drama particularly fruitful. Creative arts draw upon the power of the imagination to both remind us of the already imagined (in terms of categorical sex/gender/sexuality and behaviours) and to re-imagine new possibilities. In a recent presentation on the current state of queer teaching, Jim Sears described an exercise in queering where children are asked to create imaginary characters with traits that do not fit the contours of the heterosexual matrix (2007). We have explored the power of the transgressive imaginary elsewhere (Atkinson and DePalma, 2007), and the *No Outsiders* project provides a way to explore some specific approaches to what we have referred to as unbelieving the heterosexual matrix (Atkinson and DePalma, in press).

Jody Norton proposes that we draw upon children's innate interest in fantasy play to literally perform transgressive bodies in the classroom:

> Suppose one is less interested in removing Cinderella from children's reading lists or in marketing a PC knockoff than in offering a way of reading Perrault's version as a kaleidoscope of fantasies of transformation that might include a boy dressing up as a girl, or *becoming* a girl for the duration of the story (or at least until 'midnight')? ... why not also encourage further flights of the gendered imagination; for example, reading Cinderella as a male-bodied character, or Robin Hood (like Peter Pan) as a female-bodied one, and explaining that some children (and adults) identify fundamentally (not just transiently) across sex/gender lines; or drawing attention to alternatively gendered beings like fairies, who are not always represented as clearly either masculine or feminine? (1999, p418)

While on the one hand literature has the potential for reinforcing normative categories and hierarchies (consider beautiful but oppressed Cinderella's instantiation of the ultimate heterosexual fantasy), much of the quality of polysemic (multi-layered) texts, especially picture books, is seen to lie in their potential for subversion and inversion of the norm. Norton argues that the key to troubling, rather than reinforcing, the norm lies with how literature is used: whether children are allowed to draw upon the power of their imaginations to open, rather than close, possibilities.

In our own work we have noticed that, as Jackson and Gee point out (2005), children tend to identify with traditional hierarchies as presented in stories and resist alternative representations of these. Laura, one of our project teachers, discovered after reading *King and King* (De Haan and Nijland, 2002) that while her 8 and 9 year-old pupils were aware that Prince Bertie married one of the princesses' brothers, many children sought explanations of why he rejected the princesses, which overlooked this dénouement. Nevertheless, she found that by reading the traditional Cinderella story and then allowing children to explore alternative versions by taking on the personae of various characters and producing their own alternative version (by shifting race, class, gender and sexuality) she was able to tap into the subversive potential of the imaginary (see Allan, Atkinson, Brace, DePalma and Hemingway, 2008, for more about Laura's methods).

While Sue and Laura have both found *King and King* provides rich ground for troubling certainties about gender and sexuality, Laura has also just discovered a way to queer science within her assigned class theme of underwater sea creatures:

> Each year at [my school] the class names have a different theme and this year it is 'under the sea.' I'm rather excited ... that my class will be the seahorse class – male seahorses get pregnant and lay the eggs. I'm pleased I managed to choose the queer underwater creature! I reckon that could be a good starting point for discussion about gender roles, mummies and daddies etc!

Laura's delight in having discovered a queer underwater sea creature goes beyond the answer. How do seahorses reproduce? Males lay eggs ... but that is the beginning, not the end. The queering will happen in opening and keeping open the questions posed by this answer, by allowing them to trouble our notions of sex, gender, reproduction and parenthood.

Queering as disrupting, troubling, questioning and never resting

Recalling Letts and Sears' call to recognise and challenge our own 'categorical blinders' (1999, p5), we consider ourselves deeply implicated in the ongoing project of queering early childhood education. In this sense, our current queer action research project is as much about (re) thinking as it is about doing. There will be no definitive lesson plans or supremely queer books and resources because we think teaching queerly requires a constantly interrogative and self-critical habit of mind more than particular materials or procedures. We do not even agree among ourselves about so-called best practices and resources, but the queering seems to lie in the debate rather than the resolution.

The project supports ongoing tensions that will probably never be resolved but which need to be raised and interrogated. What happens when we publicly insist that the *No Outsiders* project has nothing to do with sex? Is it really necessary to reassure the public so vehemently that children are not learning about sex, and what kind of messages are we sending to propagate the myth of the asexual innocent child? Are we contributing to heteronormativity when we barrage children with stories exclusively depicting gay and lesbian adults in monogamous loving relationships? Are we implicitly limiting sexuality to relationships and limiting these relationships to the safe ones? Are we misrepresenting transgender issues by not explicitly addressing transgender identities, or does troubling sex, gender and sexuality advance a transgender social justice project?

Perhaps most importantly, as we begin to teach queerly or observe others teaching queerly, we begin to discover our own stuck places and hastily answered questions. It is all very well for us to analyse the ways in which a pupil's queer performance reveals our own sex/gender/ sexuality conflations, but this is not a cure or an intervention, not an end but a beginning. These tentative forays into queering primary education in the UK have suggested to us that this process is more about raising and holding questions than simply presenting new and better certainties. How can a male seahorse also be a mummy?! Can a boy in a dress bonk people on the head?! Why does Cinderella fall in love with the handsome prince?! Why does Prince Bertie not want to marry any of the princesses?! It may be that queering might be as simple – and as complex – as engaging children's own abilities to ask complex questions and to play with alternative realities. It also involves asking ourselves and each other irresolvable and disturbing questions rather than resting with easy answers.

Notes

1 Colton argues not that Tinky Winky is heterosexual, but that Teletubbies are asexual creatures.

2 The photograph of Ethel Merman hanging in Elmer's room may be interpreted by some discerning readers as suggestive, although children are not likely to have access to this cultural reference.

3 They specifically refer to the DfES document *Stand up for Us*, available at http://www. wiredforhealth.gov.uk/cat.php?catid=1101&docid=7707.

References

Allan, A, Atkinson, E, Brace, E, DePalma, R, and Hemingway, J (2008) Speaking the unspeakable in forbidden places: addressing lesbian, gay, bisexual and transgender equality in the primary school. *Sex Education* 8(3), p315-328

Atkinson, E, and DePalma, R (in press) Unbelieving the matrix: queering consensual heteronormativity. *Gender and Education*

Atkinson, E, and DePalma, R (2007) Imagining the homonormative: the place of subversive research in education for social justice. *British Journal of Sociology of Education* 29(1), p25-35

Beckett, J (2007) *The Sissy Duckling* [book review] http://www.therainbowbabies. com/TheSissyDuckling.html (July 2007)

Butler, J (1990) *Gender Trouble: feminism and the subversion of identity*. New York: Routledge

The Christian Institute (2006) *Curriculum in the Courtroom: how new laws will give activists the power to sue schools* http://www.christian.org.uk/soregs/gayright books.htm (June 2007)

Colton, M (1999) I'm sorry, Tinky Winky. *Salon Newsreel* http://www.salon.com/news/ 1999/02/13newsb.html (February 2007)

De Haan, L, and Nijland, S (2002) *King and King*. Berkeley, CA: Tricycle Press

Easton, A (2007) Poland targets 'gay' Teletubbies http://news.bbc.co.uk/2/hi/europe/ 6698753.stm (May 2007)

Fierstein, H and Cole, H (2002) *The Sissy Duckling*. London: Simon and Schuster

Jackson, S and Gee, S (2005) 'Look Janet', 'no you look John': constructions of gender in early school reader illustrations across 50 years. *Gender and Education* 17(2) p115 – 128

Letts, W and Sears, J (1999) *Queering Elementary Education: advancing the dialogue about sexualities and schooling.* Lanham: Rowman and Littlefield

Linné, R (2003) Alternative textualities: media culture and the proto-queer. *International Journal of Qualitative Studies in Education* 16(3) p669-689

Moore, R (2007) Dr. Kinsey meets Dr. Seuss: culture wars and children's literature http://www.henryinstitute.org/article_read.php?cid=15 (July, 2007)

Norton, J (1999) Transchildren and the discipline of children's literature. *The Lion and the Unicorn* 23(3) p415-436

Pharr, S (1988) *Homophobia : a weapon of sexism.* Inverness: Chardon Press

Renold, E (2005) *Girls, Boys, and Junior Sexualities: exploring children's gender and sexual relations in the primary school.* London: RoutledgeFalmer

Renold, E (2006) 'They won't let us play ... unless you're going out with one of them': girls, boys and Butler's 'heterosexual matrix' in the primary years. *British Journal of Sociology of Education* 27(4), 489-509

Sears, J (2007) Primary directives for teaching and researching on the (out)side of sexualities equalities. Paper presented at the seminar Invisible boundaries: Addressing sexualities equalities in children's worlds, Cardiff, Wales, 18 May

Walt Disney Feature Animation (1994) *The Lion King* USA

Youdell, D (2006) *Impossible Bodies, Impossible Selves: exclusions and student subjectivities.* Dordrecht: Springer

Zephaniah, B (2002) *The Little Book of Vegan Poems.* Oakland: AK Press

13

Using children's literature to challenge homophobia in primary schools

The No Outsiders Project Team

The *No Outsiders* project, funded by the Economic and Social Research Council, aims to create more inclusive primary school environments. Led by Elizabeth Atkinson and Renée DePalma at the University of Sunderland, in collaboration with researchers at the University of Exeter and the Institute of Education, University of London, the project is exploring ways of challenging homophobia and transphobia through positive and non-stereotypical representations of gay, lesbian and bisexual people, as well as people who do not conform to rigid gender stereotypes. Like those of Watkins and Sapon-Shevin, this chapter explores some concrete possibilities for classroom activities and resources, focusing specifically on one of the avenues the project team has been exploring: the use of children's books.

Schools participating in the *No Outsiders* project are using a collection of children's books featuring non-heterosexual characters. Favourites include *And Tango Makes Three* (Parnell and Richardson, 2005), the true story of two male penguins in New York's Central Park zoo who bring up a penguin chick; *King and King* (DeHaan and Nijland, 2002), about two princes who fall in love; and *Spacegirl Pukes* (Watson and Carter, 2006), about a space-travelling girl with two mums who gets a tummy bug. Many of these books carry deeper messages: for example, *One Dad, Two Dads, Brown Dad, Blue Dads* (Valentine and Sarecky, 2004) takes a wry look at the strange explanations for why people are as they are, and suggests that we should just accept them as themselves.

In one primary school, the National Literacy Strategy objective which requires pupils to write their own versions of traditional tales has provided the framework for an exploration of diverse relationships. The teacher used *King and King* as a starting point for work in which the children reconsidered the classic Cinderella-type tale and wrote alternative Cinderella stories. Drama work, with puppets made by the children, was used throughout the unit to allow the children to explore different identities for their characters. The teacher says:

> We began the lesson with a letter from the Prince asking the class for help (because he has to meet all these princesses but doesn't want to marry any of them) and then we read the book. The children then had to make puppets of their own Cinderella characters. Lots of boys decided to have male Cinderellas and a couple of boys decided to have gay characters.

As part of literacy strategy teaching in another primary school, a teacher is working with pupils to create a libretto for an opera based on two of the project books, *And Tango Makes Three* and *Oliver Button is a Sissy,* the story of a boy who loves dancing (DePaola, 1979). In a discussion with these Year 6 pupils, they told us that both books are good even for very young children because they help them understand that 'it's OK to be different'.

Mark Jennett, the project's diversity trainer, particularly likes the subtlety of texts like *Tango*. He states:

> I particularly like how *And Tango Makes Three* expresses no surprise about the nurturing instincts of the male penguins. So many books that aim to challenge stereotyping still suggest that their gentle boys or feisty girls are unusual. Interestingly, no one has asked me if I think the penguins are like this because they are gay (I don't!) but it would still make for a fascinating and, I think, wholly positive discussion if they did.

An Advanced Skills Teacher is incorporating a range of books depicting non-heterosexual-headed families and characters who resist gender stereotypes into a scheme of work for emotional literacy, and this is being used in a number of schools across two Local Authorities. One activity piloted this year involved reading the book *William's Doll* (Zolotow and DuBois, 1985), which explores the story of a small boy who wants a doll, with a group of Year 6 pupils and then inviting them to visit a reception class to observe and participate in the children's play. In the ensuing discussion about the reception children's gendered play choices, the Year 6 pupils brought up several related issues, including ways that adults might not conform to gender stereotypes, people who change from man to woman and vice versa (the teacher offered and explained the word 'transgender'), and lesbian and gay people in popular media. The teacher reports:

> The consensus at the end of the discussion was that it was our responsibility to challenge incidents where we saw people being pressured into gender stereotypes ... Once we had got past the stock 'It's what's inside that counts' answers, we were able to talk about peer pressure and its effect on all of us.

In a small rural church school, a selection of books were used as the focus for work across the whole school for a *No Outsiders* inclusion week, with the pupils presenting some of their work for parents in the village church at the end of the week. Years 5 and 6 studied *The Harvey Milk Story* (Krakow and Gardner, 2002), the biography of the first openly gay US elected representative, who was murdered because he was gay.

Year 1 and 2 adapted *King and King* into a pantomime and introduced two new characters, a fairy godmother and a wicked doctor. They also read the sequel, *King and King and Family* (DeHaan and Nijland, 2004), in which the two princes, now happily married, adopt a baby girl. They wrote wedding invitations for the princes' wedding and travel journals from their honeymoon as part of their literacy hour work.

The Reception class listened to *And Tango Makes Three*, talked about different family patterns and created a penguin dance. Earlier in the year, *And Tango Makes Three* and *We Do: a celebration of gay and lesbian marriage* – a book of photographs celebrating lesbian and gay weddings – (Newsom and Rennert, 2004) were used to discuss family patterns and civil partnerships after one of the Reception children said her two mothers were getting married to each other. Sue, the school's headteacher, says:

> The funny thing was that although the children enjoyed working with these stories, they didn't seem overly bothered by the explicit references to LGBT issues/same sex parents/gay ducks – they loved the stories for what they are – stories!

The *No Outsiders* project team has held workshops using these books around the country, both within and beyond the regions in which the project is taking place. The books have been enthusiastically received. The participants frequently declared that they would be buying copies for their own schools or organisations. In the follow-up to one workshop, Renée, who co-leads the project, commented on reactions to *The Sissy Duckling* (Fierstein and Cole, 2002), a tale of a duckling who loves cooking, cleaning and art, hates sports, and rescues his wounded father, using his skills to survive the winter when the rest of the flock has flown away:

> [Some of the workshop participants] pointed out that it reinforces some stereotypes – the cover is full of glitter, the duckling is a sissy because he cooks, keeps house, etc. And I could completely see the validity of these critiques. But I would worry that this might be [presented as] an argument for *not* using the book, which I think would short-circuit a great opportunity to discuss with kids whether the books reinforce stereotypes and how that might happen ... I believe that even very small children are capable of having that kind of discussion, and it's even more useful than using a book that you see as so perfect there's no room for critical discussion.

The books have been warmly welcomed by teachers participating in the project. In one Local Authority, the project booklist has become part of the new guidance for primary schools on challenging homophobia. The PSHE adviser who put the guidance together says:

> The books are excellent for examining identity and difference in a non-threatening context. They break down what we as adults would consider difficult issues into manageable age-appropriate narratives.

One primary headteacher taking part in the project says:

> These books have at last given us a familiar vehicle through which to discuss issues of equalities and sexualities, based around ideas of families and relationships, with young children. They are an invaluable resource in our school.

Another primary headteacher says:

> I particularly like *King and King* because you could use it with a whole range of age groups. The illustrations are very good, and both illustrations and text are easy to access – and it's fun! You could explore alternative endings to fairytales with it, and it lends itself well to drama and PSHE work. We have so many different types of families that schools need to take a good hard look at themselves and ask, do we really represent the society which the children

are living in? These books offer us the opportunity to have a dialogue with children about families.

And yet another primary headteacher had this to say:

Teachers have used the project books in story sessions during the week and class assemblies linked to PSHCE. Our school serves a diverse community where children come from assorted family arrangements; there are many single parents, extended families from a range of cultural backgrounds, looked-after children, those in differing step families and some families with same-sex parenting ... At a basic level the books affirm this diversity. For some it gives them confidence that their own circumstances are shared by others. Even in our school many children feel pressure to conform and a consequence of this is for children to keep quiet about those aspects that might make them seem different. Books give credibility to what may seem unusual to others.

Overall, this collection of books has provided a set of tools for exploring key issues around identity and diversity for *all* children, whatever their particular family circumstances or whatever their future sexual orientation. Participating teachers have commented that using these books has opened up discussions about the whole range of family patterns which exist in contemporary society. This is a discussion which has for too long been silenced – to the detriment of any children who might feel that, for one reason or another, they don't quite 'fit in'.

For more information about the *No Outsiders* project, and an annotated list of books for children featuring non-heterosexual characters and addressing issues of identity and diversity, see the project website: www.nooutsiders.sunderland.ac.uk. To order copies of the project books, contact sales@gaystheword.co.uk.

References

DeHaan, L and Nijland, S (2002) *King and King.* Berkeley, CA: Tricycle Press

DeHaan, L and Nijland, S (2004) *King and King and Family.* Berkeley, CA: Tricycle Press

DePaola, T (1979) *Oliver Button is a Sissy.* San Diego, CA: Harcourt Trade Publishers

Fierstein, H and Cole, H (2002) *The Sissy Duckling.* London: Simon and Schuster

Krakow, K and Gardner, D (2002) T*he Harvey Milk Story.* Ridley Park, PA: Two Lives Publishing

Newsom, G and Rennert, A (2004) *We Do: a celebration of gay and lesbian marriage.* San Francisco: Chronicle Books

Parnell, P and Richardson, J (2005) *And Tango Makes Three.* New York: Simon and Schuster Children's Publishing

Valentine, J and Sarecky, M (2004) *One Dad, Two Dads, Brown Dad, Blue Dads.* Los Angeles, CA: Alyson Books

Watson, K and Carter, V (2006) *Space Girl Pukes.* London: Onlywomen Press

Zolotow, C and DuBois, W (1985) *William's Doll.* New York: HarperTrophy

Notes on contributors

Maryam Al-Alami is Associate Lecturer and graduate student at Manchester Metropolitan University, School of Law and holds a Master's degree from the University of Nottingham. In 2007 she collaborated with Stephen Whittle and Lewis Turner on *Engendered Penalties: Transgender and Transsexual People's Experiences of Inequality and Discrimination* (Crown Copyright 2007), a research project and report commissioned by the Equalities Review. This project, based on the largest data collection ever analysed and the largest survey response ever received when doing research on trans people's lives, outlines the levels of inequality and discrimination that trans people face.

Elizabeth Atkinson is a Reader in Social and Educational Inquiry and Co-Director of the Centre for Equalities and Social Justice at the University of Sunderland. Until 2007, she was the European regional editor of the *International Journal of Qualitative Studies in Education*. She has published widely on lesbian, gay, bisexual and transgender identities and equalities in primary school settings and in 2007 was awarded the Queer Studies Scholar Activist award by the Queer Studies Special Interest Group of the American Educational Research Association. Elizabeth is the Director of the ESRC-funded *No Outsiders* project (www. nooutsiders.sunderland.ac.uk) which supports UK primary teachers, in collaboration with three universities, in exploring strategies to challenge heteronormativity and address sexualities equality in their own professional settings.

Renée DePalma received her PhD in 2003 from the University of Delaware (US), where she developed and taught modules on equality and diversity for primary teacher trainees. In 1997 she helped establish the university-community partnership *La Red Magica* with the Latin American Community Center in Wilmington, Delaware. Her research and teaching has focused on social justice and equity in terms of ethnicity, language, race, gender and sexuality. Renée has been working at the University of Sunderland (UK) in sexualities equality research since 2004, and is currently working as Research Fellow for the *No Outsiders* project (www.

nooutsiders.sunderland.ac.uk). She is a founding member of the Centre for Equalities and Social Justice at the University of Sunderland (UK) and book reviews editor for the journal *Power and Education* (Symposium Journals).

Catherine Donovan is a Reader in Sociology at the University of Sunderland where she has been for 12 years. She teaches the sociology of gender, family and sexuality; and the sociology of health and the body. She has conducted research in non-heterosexual communities for 17 years. This has included studies of the ways in which lesbians are able to access donor insemination; how gay men who are HIV+ engage in safer sex; families of choice; and more recently, domestic abuse in same-sex and heterosexual relationships. She is the co-author of *Families of Choice and other Life Experiments* (2001) (with Jeffrey Weeks and Brian Heaphy) which reported on the biggest study of LGB intimate and family relationships in the UK to date; and co-editor (with Angelia Wilson) of a special edition of the journal *Sexualities*, exploring same-sex parenting. Catherine is currently the project manager of an evaluation of the NRF funded Domestic Abuse Intervention Programme in the North East and Cumbria and the Director of the International Centre for the Study of Violence and Abuse based within the School of Health, Natural and Social Sciences at the University.

Debbie Epstein is a semi-retired, part-time professor at Cardiff School of Social Sciences. She is also a part time psychotherapist in training, registered with the United Kingdom Council for Psychotherapy, and practices in Cardiff and Wotton-under-Edge. She has published extensively on issues of sexuality, gender, race and their intersections in educational sites and popular culture. Much of this work has been with Richard Johnson, most significantly, *Schooling Sexualities* (1998). Most recently, she has been working with colleagues on questions of gender and sexuality in the context of HIV and the AIDS pandemic in South Africa and their book, *Intervening against the Odds. gender equality and schooling in the context of HIV and AIDS*, will be published by the University of KwaZulu-Natal Press.

Jo Frankham is Senior Lecturer in Education in the School of Education at the University of Manchester. Her interests include interpretive approaches to educational inquiry and researching sensitive issues. Her PhD focused on sexualities education and HIV prevention education. Recent work has included an ESRC funded exploration of the rhetoric of 'partnership research' with service users and Joseph Rowntree Foundation research with children/young people who have been permanently excluded from school. Recent publications appear in *British Educational Research Journal and Journal of Education Policy*. Jo also leads the taught doctorate (EdD) in the School of Education.

Kate Hinton has a wide range of experience in education, mainly teaching in London comprehensive schools and working as a Local Authority Adviser/ Inspector in the North East of England and Scotland. She has combined a dual career path in science education and the equalities field. Based on her personal commitment, Kate has always sought opportunities to address equality issues and has held full-time equality posts at senior levels, where she has played a leading role in developing educational policy and promoting appropriate practice. Recently, that has particularly included school-level implications of the latest legislation in the related areas of gender equality and sexual orientation.

Claire Jenkins decided to leave a successful career in teaching in 1992 to change the direction of her life. Keenly interested in personal social and health education, having recently successfully completed a year-long research project on sex education for Nottinghamshire Health Authority, she began a new career by gaining a postgraduate diploma at Nottingham Trent University in Psycho-therapy and Counselling. More significantly, she embarked on a change of gender and embodiment that involved major medical, social and legal changes. She is an active and respected member of her local multicultural community. She works through the National Union of Teachers (NUT) developing LGBT issues within education and in the church developing progressive Christianity in Britain. She has delivered training in gender identity for community organisations, the local authority and universities. She has worked as a director of Relate and as an employment specialist in the Citizens Advice Bureau. She recently gained an MA with a dissertation studying transsexual transition in the film *Transamerica* and is currently a PhD student at Sheffield University.

Richard Johnson is now retired as a professor of cultural studies at Nottingham Trent University, though he continues to supervise doctoral students there. He has turned his attention to activism in relation to education and peace and is involved in the exploration of masculinities with other men in his area. From 1980-1987 he was Director of the Centre of Contemporary Cultural Studies at Birmingham University. He has published on a wide range of topics, ranging from methods for cultural studies, through cultural histories of education, nation and national identity, to sexuality and gender.

Lesbian and Gay Youth Manchester (LGYM: www.lgym.org.uk) is a Lesbian, Gay and Bisexual (LGB) Project based in the city centre for LGBs aged 14 to 25. They provide a safe space for LGB young people to feel safe and at ease in. They also provide activities for young LGBs, such as rock climbing, canoeing, cycling and walking. They do arts and craft-based work, for example banner making for Europride, environmental art and painting, and try to arrange residentials at least three times a year. They have strong links to other organisations, both LGB and non-LGB, opening up opportunities to do even more than what is on offer at LGYM. Young people have a big say in activities that go on during group time. Oh yes ... and membership to LGYM is free!

Sue Sanders is currently co-chair of Schools OUT (www.schools-out.org.uk) and instigated LGBT History Month in the UK (www.lgbthistorymonth.org). She is member of the LGBT advisory group to the Metropolitan Police, an Independent Advisor to the London Criminal Justice Board and the Race for Justice Home Office steering group and a member of the Southwark Anti-Homophobic Forum and the National Union of Teachers LGBT working group. The DfES commissioned her as exhibitor and speaker at the nine regional launches of the Anti-Bullying Charter, to raise the issues of homophobic bullying. She worked with the CPS on their policy and guidance on prosecuting Homophobic and Transphobic crime and, with Dr Michael Halls, co-trains all the CPS LGBT liaison officers across the country. Sue co-wrote a teacher's pack for Tackling Homophobia, Creating Safer Spaces, a model Equal Opportunity and Anti-Bullying Policy for Schools. Along with Paul Patrick, Sue co-founded CHRYSALIS (http://www.thechrysalisteam.co.uk), a team of trainers that delivers work on diversity and particularly LGBT issues.

Mara Sapon-Shevin is Professor of Inclusive Education in the Teaching and Leadership Department of the School of Education at Syracuse University (US). Mara writes extensively about the fields of full inclusion, cooperative learning, social justice education and teaching for diversity. Her book *Because We Can Change the World: a practical guide for building cooperative, inclusive classroom communities* (Allyn and Bacon, 1998) explores ways in which teachers can use cooperative games, children's literature, music and curriculum to build classroom communities which model inclusion and acceptance. Her most recent book is *Widening the Circle: the power of inclusive classrooms* (Boston: Beacon Press, 2007). Mara works with anti-racism and anti-homophobia projects in the community with students, teachers and faculty. She is co-author of a seven session anti-racism curriculum entitled, 'Endracism/Endinjustice: Challenging Oppression, Building Allies' and the co-producer of a DVD entitled *And Nobody Said Anything: uncomfortable conversations about diversity*. Mara also sings and dances inclusively for social justice (www.marasapon-shevin.org).

Jay Stewart is co-founder of Gendered Intelligence, a company set up to use arts-based programmes to work with young trans people. He was the documentary maker for the Sci:dentity Project (March 2006-March 2007). His latest film, produced in collaboration with the *No Outsiders* project, features some of the experiences of young trans people in primary school and is designed for teachers to use as a training tool. Jay facilitates film-making projects to community groups as well as tutoring and lecturing on various undergraduate and postgraduate units. He is an active member of the trans community, having chaired FTM London, a support group for transmen, from October 2004 to March 2007. He sits on various committees and working groups, such as Sexual Orientation and Gender Identity Advisory Group and the Trans@Pride sub-committee. Jay's academic interests lie within Trans Studies and visual culture. His PhD investigates understandings of the 'real' in relation to trans. One area of concern here is within documentary filmmaking where *being real* or *being taken seriously as the 'real thing'* is central to the genre and codification of the documentary itself.

Lewis Turner is involved in research, training and consultancy for Press For Change, the leading authority on trans people and the law. Along with Stephen Whittle, he recently undertook research commissioned by the International Lesbian and Gay Association Europe (ILGA) on the experiences of trans people accessing healthcare in Europe. They were recently commissioned by the Centre for Excellence in Leadership (CEL) to produce a toolkit for FE colleges entitled *Leading Trans Equality: a Toolkit for Colleges.* Turner has published academic papers and research reports on race equality, diversity and governance as well as gender recognition and the law. His PhD thesis, funded by the Economic and Social Research Council, was the first ethnographic study of a transgender group in the UK. Turner is Hate Crimes Officer for Wyre Borough Council, working with Lancashire Police. He is a member of a Hate Crime Scrutiny Panel for the Crown Prosecution Service and a member of the Association of Chief Police Officers (ACPO) Trans portfolio group. He trains Lancashire Constabulary student officers on trans issues.

Mark Vicars is a Senior Lecturer in Literacy Education at the University of Victoria, Melbourne, Australia. He was the recipient of an ESRC PhD Scholarship in the Department of Educational Studies, University of Sheffield, UK. His doctoral research investigated the formative reading practices and literacy behaviour of gay men. He has published a number of papers and book chapters which have appeared or are in press in *Sex Education, Auto/Biography, British Educational Research Journal, Pedagogy, Culture and Society, Literacy and Social Inclusion and Researching Education from the Inside*, all in the areas of literacy and sexuality. He has recently been awarded a grant to investigate LGBT discrimination in FE institutions.

David Watkins is a Key Stage 3 teacher in a special school in London. In 2008, he achieved national attention by becoming the first teacher to take a school and its governors to tribunal over breach of the Sexual Orientations Regulations 2003. The positive result has since informed equal opportunities in the borough. He now enjoys a positive inclusive working environment and sits on the Equalities

Steering Committee at his current school. He has had his work on tackling homophobia published on the General Teaching Council website and has recently contributed to a Terrence Higgins Trust Resource into teaching about homosexuality in Key Stage 4. His articles on LGBT inclusivity and role models for boys have appeared in the NUT magazine *The Teacher* and the PSHE journal *Learning for Life*. In May 2008 David featured in the documentary 'School Matters: Gay Teachers' by Lambent Productions for Teachers TV (www.teachers.tv).

Stephen Whittle OBE is professor of equalities law at Manchester Metropolitan University. He is a founder and vice-president of Press For Change (http://www. pfc.org.uk), which campaigns for respect and equality for all trans people. He is also co-ordinator of the UK's support network for 'female to male' trans people (http://www.ftm.org.uk). He transitioned from female to male himself in the mid-1970s, having come from a background of Women's Liberation and Gay Liberation politics, and has retained the feminist and queer political views he developed then. Recent publications include *The Transgender Studies Reader* (Taylor and Francis, 2006) with Susan Stryker, and the research report *Transgender Euro Study: Legal Survey and Focus on the Transgender Experience of Health Care* (April 2008), with Lewis Turner, Ryan Combs and Stephenne Rhodes. The report, commissioned by ILGA-Europe is available at http://www. ilga-europe.org/europe/publications.

Index

For enquiries or renewal at
Quarles LRC
Tel: 01708 455011 – Extension 4009